Odiyan Country Cookbook

Odiyan

Country

Cookbook

Bill Farthing

Dharma

Acknowledgements

This book is dedicated to Tarthang Tulku, Rinpoche. Without his inspiration, teaching, and example, it could not have been written. For these gifts we are deeply thankful. Thanks to Edna Katz, whose critical ear and good sense of humor contributed greatly to the editing. Our thanks to Endy Stark, Jane Harrer, and Rhonda Karlton for their recipes and experience in cooking; to Debbie Black, Evelyn Foster, and Millan Trench for their knowledge of Tibetan cooking; to Tom Chakas for his tofu experiments, Richard Katz for his encouragement of healthful cooking, and Jerry A. Berg for his skill in sharpening knives; to Sandi Ray for typesetting; to Betty Cook, Sally Sorenson, and Judy Rasmussen for their ability to decipher and type handwriting; to Peter Ogilvie for his photography, Mirriam Hersey for her graphics assistance, and Rosalyn White for her cover painting; to Denise Anderson for her assistance in testing these recipes this summer, proofreading, and line drawings; our thanks to Merrill Peterson for his editorial work, design, layout, and advice about content. Our appreciation to the members of Dharma Publishing and Dharma Press for their work in printing and binding this volume.

Photos by Peter Ogilvie, drawings by Denise Anderson, cover by Rosalyn White

Typeset in Fototronic Century Schoolbook and Windsor
printed and bound by Dharma Press, Emeryville, California

9 8 7 6 5 4 3

Foreword

This is a cookbook for people who enjoy being alive, who enjoy experimenting, and who are open to change. It is for people who care about themselves and want to learn to prepare nourishing meals in a confident and conscious manner. The purpose of the book is to help us achieve a balance within and between ourselves and the earth when we prepare food. It calls attention to the life in food and to the cycles of energy transmitted from the earth through food to the individual and back again. Each culture has a different appreciation of the universe which includes a special understanding of food, its preparation, and the way it is eaten. This book is a compilation of aesthetic and nourishing recipes from many cultures which incorporate some of their age-old beliefs about healthful cooking and eating. It includes recipes which are new in taste, in their combinations, and in their methods of preparation.

Many influences combined to create this book. It began very simply. People who have participated in the seminars and classes at the Nyingma Institute in Berkeley and the community working at Odiyan, a country retreat center, enjoyed the meals to the extent that we have had many in-

quiries for recipes. Over the years we began to refine our methods and thought we would make copies of each menu, available on request. Then we decided to compile our favorites. Finally, we decided to go beyond menus and include the total experience of cooking as an art of growth and communication.

Many of the recipes in this book are a record of the varied journeys we have taken toward the recognition that what is healthful and what is delicious are the same. We think that these recipes will please both the traditional and the more health-conscious cook because our approach to diet is a straightforward attempt to prepare food in such a way that the body and psyche are invigorated and nourished.

The food we cook at Odiyan tends to be very simple, especially when so many naturally delicious vegetables are available from our garden. Although our chickens produce many eggs, we are essentially dependent on a correct balance of grains and beans or soy-dairy products to provide protein. As we cook we improvise to suit our feelings and the materials at hand. It is our wish to pass on those rare moments of perfection. We hope that you will consult these recipes with this same spirit, and that

some of them will broaden the areas of your experimentation and delight, too.

A few of these recipes include alternate suggestions of meat stocks or fish, and there are recipes with meat in the section on "Food from the Top of the World". Our diet is almost completely vegetarian, but we do eat meat or fish on occasion. Our goal is a knowledgeable and balanced diet that is responsive to all of our needs rather than to any particular cultural conditioning. As Nagarjuna writes:

By knowing that food is like medicine
May you rely on it without cupidity or
    avarice.
It is not for power, nor for pride.
It is not for mental inflation, but is
    only to support your body.

After all, there are more important things than food! When our diet is healthful and encourages us to open our senses, then we can begin the really important work of understanding our minds.

Contents

Odiyan Country Cookbook

Introduction

The Cook

To be a cook is to have a primal, almost magical role. We become a link between the transformative vitality of this living earth and the world of man and his fictions. Since the disparity between these two areas of life is often extreme, it is important that we wake up to the very profound impact our own awareness can have on the quality of our lives.

Cooking is a primary art, not just because it can be such a simple activity, but because it embraces so much of life. Each meal is different even if it uses the same ingredients, just as we are different with each passing moment. Our experience is actually unique each time we cook, and each meal is an original expression of our very being. Most of us think of cooking as just preparing a meal, but when we *really* cook, it is a simple celebration.

To be able to cook creatively, even when we don't feel like it, can be a real secret. The heart of this secret lies in each moment we cook, and is found with a relaxed body and open senses. To be so receptive to our experience that we can truly appreciate exactly what we are doing is the key and fulfillment of cooking. When we are open in this way, just this simple wholeness is already nutrition. The directness, depth, and clarity of our attention is the catalyst that releases the meaning in our personal experience and the potency in our art.

Real cooking asks of us one simple thing: that we approach the food we intend to prepare with the readiness to be changed ourselves. When we restrict our awareness in an effort to become efficient and impersonal, whether to follow a recipe or just to get the job done, the life that is happening around and within us can become a nuisance. The cook becomes dull, the cooking a chore, and the raw foods so dead and characterless that we spend our time trying to manipulate them into something else that is edible. When this kind of activity takes place in the kitchen nothing can be alive—and certainly not the cook!

If we become so fixated by our expectations of what *ought* to be that we can no longer tell what *is* happening, then we are lost. Some people become so preoccupied by their expectations that they lose their spontaneity and confidence and become helpless without a book. If you walk into the kitchen and ask them what they have just done, they may have to consult the cookbook to tell you! So they aren't really alive to their own experience, and unfortunately, the laboriously prepared food is only half-awake too. How we approach the total act of cooking affects not only the food we prepare, but also the lives of those we feed.

The saying goes that "we are what we eat." This includes not only the raw foods but also their preparation—and the quality of their preparation is determined by the cook's attention to his or her own personal experience. If we truly intend to feed other people, then our experience certainly should be alive enough to stimulate and refresh ourselves. It can be very helpful to remember that the more receptive we are to the totality of our experience, the more energy there will be to receive and thus to transmit. Food communicates that energy through the quality of our preparation. It is this personal energy, as well as the natural energy in the food, that people receive.

To cook is to transform energy, whether we understand this as a process of heating beans or experience it as a creative state of mind. When we respect the pristine individuality of live foods, the pots, the stove, the being of people around us—then we are beginning to *cook*. If we can also continue to respect the simple integrity of each moment we spend cooking, then our experience can truly open. There is really nothing else to attain. When the cook is completely open to his experience, cooking becomes an art; and perhaps in more ways than many other arts, his activity becomes a transmission of consciousness to other human beings.

Cooking

What is cooking? The turnips could be anywhere, but the cook is surely in the pot. Feeling like we are right in the kettle is a very common experience and sometimes is not that pleasant. There are two Japanese proverbs to the effect that the cook should protect the vegetables as he would his own eyesight, and consider the kettle to be his own head. Since it is the case that we *are* cooking, the first thing we need to do is to take a deep breath and relax.

If the cook approaches the kitchen with the intention of enjoying himself, then organization, pleasure, and aesthetics can follow. The organization the cook brings to the kitchen is particularly essential because it allows him to relax. It may be helpful to sketch out the menu a few days to a week in advance. This helps us to develop a sense of how one meal dovetails with the next in terms of nutrition and aesthetics. Organization also strengthens our capacity to respond flexibly and confidently to changing situations. It gives us the freedom to direct the flow of our experience in the kitchen.

This approach enables us to enter the kitchen refreshed because we have done our extensive planning and thinking beforehand. When it is time to cook we can trust our senses and intuition with confidence. Our energy can be fresh and we can take our time in getting to know the live foods themselves. If we are patient, we may find that the vegetables will teach us how they may be brought to their own best expression at that moment. This kind of thoroughness can free us to the point where we can completely devote ourselves to the improvisational dialectic of real cooking.

Cooking is actually a simple ceremony. Things are happening: the cook greets the food, the food opens to the cook, and the cook opens to the cooking. If our hearts are open, then our meeting is complete and pure.

Such a meeting happens in a very special place. The cook always creates the space in which he works. It can be helpful to organize the kitchen to make this very clear. For instance, the utensils may be placed where they are immediately accessible, yet conveniently out of the way. Perhaps we would like to create an open horizon of counters and work tables that are kept clear so there is a feeling of openness and expansion. Or, it may be our style to work in a small grotto surrounded by ferns, stones, and candlelight. When we have a sense of private space, it is easy to keep the kitchen clean between each step of the cooking process. We can allow ourselves to concentrate on the activity that is transpiring at each moment. We can also create psychological space for ourselves in acknowledging that each step of the process has a beginning and an end. Even though we may be in the middle of preparing a meal, a clean kitchen can help us to remember that the next thing we do, we are really doing for the first time. The sense of returning to beginnings allows us to renew

ourselves and open up to the unseen qualities of our experience. A child will remove his toys from the toybox and place them on the floor around him with complete precision. He communicates wonder because the order he creates is his own drama. If the cook would assemble the ingredients for the food with the same natural precision, the space in which he or she meets them would be special because it would always be unique.

A good cook can be aware of everything that is happening in the kitchen all the time. We hear the water boiling—is it boiling too fast?—is energy being wasted? The sound of the vegetables being chopped—too loud? Is someone angry? Or is the knife too dull—or are the apples just too hard? We can sense how the vegetables are cooking by listening. And our ears are open to all the sounds that reach us through the fresh air coming through the windows.

Our eyes, rather than our intentions, can best tell us how to proceed in preparing a salad. Just looking at the vegetables and their natural beauty shows us how to cut them in order to reveal their unique character. Cook with their shape and color. Their texture indicates how large and thick to slice them. We can blend a dressing to complement the salad because we know that there will never be another salad like this one again.

To make full use of our senses is to celebrate. Celebration is like play, because we are continually returning to fresh experience for our orientation, rather than to the constraints of past intentions and future expectations. Attention that unreservedly accepts the moment is the energy of creativity.

Tasting is likely to be the cook's favorite sense. A good baker knows what raw wheat tastes like. He or she tastes the rye flour that has just been ground, and the dough which he is kneading, because that is what develops his skill in baking bread which is vital in flavor and nutrition.

Simply concentrating on tasting can open up many other doors of perception. Flavors take time to disclose themselves to our senses. The flavor of a good sauce is like a song. Professional tasters are never allowed to swallow anything they are tasting because it interferes with their ability to *listen* to the taste. If you are tasting a sauce and want to know what to do next, just listen.

The flavors of food have a distinct beginning, middle, and end. Most people prefer a sauce with a strong middle and a mellow ending. A strong beginning and a great finale may taste raw without a smooth and subtle middle to tie it together. A rich lamb and vegetable curry can be a whole opera. So if you taste as if you were appreciating a musical score, your skill in cooking will improve. Good seasoning involves choosing a particular accent not only for its own unique flavor but also because it lends its character to the sauce at a definite time.

The fact that food discloses its composition to the taste sequentially can be called the breadth of its flavor. The breadth is mostly composed of aromatic essences that are really smelled. There is another factor to flavor which we can call its depth. This dimension has five elements: salt, sour, sweet, hot, and bitter. These are the only flavors that the tongue can taste. (Hot, like cayenne, is smelled, too, but it can also burn the tongue.) These are the elements that literally make the mouth water. Potatoes and other starches have only a little natural depth and just require salt. On the other hand, many green vegetables have quite a lot of depth. Mustard greens, for example, may have too much. If their bitterness and hotness is balanced with the sharpness of salt and the sourness of vinegar, we may enjoy them. Some people don't like vegetables because they are used to eating them with their natural depth overcooked and diluted away. However, if we can balance a vegetable's depth, its natural aromatic flavor will often be appreciated.

Remember that most food seasoning is an attempt either to emphasize or to complement flavors already naturally present in the food. In the current wave of "gourmet" cooking many cooks tend to over-season. This is probably because many people are just learning what natural herbs taste like. In the *haute cuisines* of the world, the attempt is to balance flavors so carefully that their seasonings are almost indistinguishable. We may be enjoying the food with its mysterious sauce— simply because we are enticed to attend to the experience of tasting. In this book, however, some of the following recipes are undoubtedly overseasoned. Living in the country, we find this can be a form of entertainment. So, season to taste and the appreciation of others.

Our skill in cooking seems to grow in four basic areas. The first three areas of learning are appreciating the natural quality of raw foods, understanding their contribution to nutrition, and seasoning them to awaken our appreciation of their value. As our experience deepens, we begin to develop balance. This fourth area of growth is the expression of our knowledge and sensitivity. It is the factor that makes the difference between a meal that is just a collection of dishes and a meal that is a unified and living whole. When such a meal is eaten, people are well-nourished, content and happy. They feel light, rather than stuffed, and their senses are awakened during digestion instead of being put to sleep. Often people will eat surprisingly little at such a meal because each dish combines to nourish the psyche as well as the body.

Once we are able to design a menu in which the dishes complement one another in texture, color, flavor, and nutrition, we can begin to practice balance as we cook. The secret of this skill is lightness. It helps to think of the food as nearly weightless, and to imagine the food to be composed entirely of visible light. At the same time, the lighter and more sensitive our feeling tone, the more we may be working with the nutritional energies themselves.

We can also let the dishes relate to each other as we cook. For example, as you stir-fry green beans and onions, try to visualize the peas and new potatoes you have just prepared. When one dish is cooked "with" another in this way, our creativity may surprise us in responding with new seasonings and new compositions.

The whole meal unfolds gradually as the cooks opens to the influences that the ingredients have upon each other. If the cook is able to keep in touch with this developing wholeness, a dance emerges as the ingredients arrange themselves in new patterns and flavors. When the cook becomes the meeting place for the energies of nutrition, the meal balances itself. The cook is open to new energies too, and he or she is recombined with new seasonings right along with the food.

Food

A *good* cook so trusts his senses that he is free to discover what good food really is. The *best* cook is a person who has taken this awakening process one step further through paying attention to how each food affects his body. He learns to cook with the essential messages and energies that foods bring to his whole health.

Cooking does not stop after the food is put on the table. Food continues to cook in the body, which is the most sensitive and exacting cook of all. The number of processes required to break down, recombine, and assimilate our food are almost beyond comprehension. Of course, we do not have to be aware of these processes for them to work, but perhaps we can appreciate that the body can handle huge amounts of information with incredible sensitivity, speed, and precision. Our bodies are profoundly aware. What is astonishing is that

our civilization encourages us to think of our bodies as just another machine or material object. When this is our attitude, it is a matter of course to ignore our health.

Our health becomes more important to us when we begin to recognize that our experience is the unity of the interrelationship between our minds and our bodies. The more we accept this wholeness the more natural it is for us to recognize our bodies as real teachers. It makes just as much sense for us to prepare pure foods that nourish our bodies as it does to discover the truths that nourish our minds.

Natural whole foods have an internal balance which is usually destroyed in commercial processing. This distortion can be introduced into our own systems, especially when inorganic additives (including large amounts of refined sugars and salts) are present. If the cook can find natural foods and organic vegetables he or she will be offering the body a whole and pure message.

Every food has its proper use. For those of us interested in learning more about what specific kinds of diets are healthful, there are many books available with useful suggestions that can be pursued. However, to choose a new diet purely from intellectual conviction may not be very helpful, unless we are also willing to listen to what our bodies have to tell us about our choices.

It is important to read about nutrition because that knowledge can be a good guide. However, we do not need to rely wholly on the *concepts* of vitamins and proteins when we can experience the communication directly with the food. Trusting the information our bodies provide is essential to health.

Our bodies reveal the subtle energies in food. When we use all our senses in cooking, including the *whole body*, we may discover that "carrot", for example, is something more than what is revealed by its taste. We may experience it as a factor in energizing pure vision and in sharpening our concentration. Respecting the experience of "cooking with our whole body" develops a balanced and accurate intuitive sense about selecting and preparing nourishing food. We can know that what we communicate is indeed as positive as we intend. Certainly this is a very essential contribution to the quality of life around us.

Eating

Gather your friends around the table and bring forth the supper. The simple fact of eating together turns strangers into friends and friends into family. It is a time of sharing life. Like other forms of sharing, it is often deepest in silence. When we relax and carefully taste our food it is also a natural occasion for thankfulness. Eating slowly allows the time to appreciate the simple majesty in the flow of energy from distant fields through the fires of the hearth and into our senses. Eating is like accepting a gift or learning how to take a compliment. When we completely open to the pleasure of receiving, then, in that moment, we are giving all there is to give.

Our capacity to receive and to be nourished is truly important in this existence. The acceptance and love we have for ourselves is the foundation of our growth.

Not Eating

Those of us who have never intentionally fasted have missed a very beneficial opportunity to renew ourselves. To continually load, or overload, our bodies with food is to misuse our digestive system. From time to time it needs a rest. Our bodies accumulate toxins from the food we eat and from our own physiological processes. The poisons in our bloodstream can be especially high when our diet is unbalanced, impure, or too rich. Abstaining from consuming everything but water is an ancient way to fast, and is almost certain to be completely safe for everyone in reasonably good health.

If you would like to fast, choose a time when you will not be engaged in unusually strenuous work. It is a good idea to gradually eliminate refined sweets and heavy starches from your diet during the week before you begin. The last day before the fast drink only fruit and vegetable juices and other light liquids.

The fast may last from four days to a month; two weeks, however, is generally an adequate amount of time to rest our organs and to remove the toxins. The body will be able to use food that has been stored in its tissues to provide energy. As the fast proceeds, the energy that was used to assimilate foods may assist in removing poisons if you remember to drink plenty of water. You may find that you gradually need less water, but be sure to drink when you are thirsty. Don't confuse fasting with mortification. It's simply a way to let the body rest.

It is time to stop fasting, regardless of your intentions, when the body provides either of these two signals: when you are *extremely* hungry, or, when the mucous coating on the tongue disappears. This is simply a natural communication to the effect that the fast has been successful.

When you decide to break the fast, be sure to reintroduce yourself to food very gradually. The first meal may be a little fruit juice, the second meal soup and toast. Keep your meals light for the first few days and your digestive system will awaken gradually and smoothly. Be conscious of how you respond to different foods as you reintroduce them. If you can return to a more purified and balanced diet, much of the heightened circulation, awareness, and vitality that you have experienced during the fast may be preserved.

Odiyan

Odiyan is a community being built by Tibetan Lama Tarthang Tulku on a redwood forested mountain above the Pacific Ocean in northwestern Sonoma County, California. Together with the Tibetan Nyingma Meditation Center, founded in 1969, Dharma Publishing, the Nyingma Institute, and the Tibetan Aid Project, it is one of his five major goals materializing in America. A community center has been built during the past two years inspired by traditional Tibetan architecture. A picture of it can be seen through the window on the front cover. The central building is a mandala aligned to the four directions. It consists of a residential rim structure with four domed entryways, which form a square around a large open garden that will contain the meditation hall.

Our vision of Odiyan includes a community of homes for families and schools for children. There will be facilities for Tibetans to live and preserve their traditional arts and crafts. In our gardens and orchards we are learning to become agriculturally self-sufficient. We plan to construct facilities for medical practice and research and libraries to support translation and academic studies. To this end, income from this book will go to Odiyan.

Odiyan (O-dee-yahn) is a transliteration of the Sanskrit name for the birthplace of Padmasambhava, the great teacher who brought Buddhism to Tibet.

Menus

The Menus which follow are suggestions for ways of combining the recipes in this book which we have found to be particularly successful. A sustaining diet certainly does not need to be so rich as this, but for shorter, festive periods, it is a pleasure.

Lunch

Tomato, Cucumber and Basil Salad
Avocado Avgolemeno
Italian Cheese and Mushroom Pie
Steam-Braised Scallop Squash
   with White Wine
Fresh Berries
Maté Tea

Oven-Pot Egg Flower Broth
Steamed Baos
Vietnamese Salad
Jelled Sesame-Apricot Cream
Green Tea

Spinach and Feta Salad
Crêpes Filled with Celery and Cheese
Rosemarie and Peas
Brandied Granola Bars
Iced Tea

Radish and Sour Cream Salad
Green Salad with Sprouts
Rich-Nut Tabouleh
Arab Bread
Turkish Almond Custard
Peppermint Tea

Aguacata Picante
Iced Yogurt Soup
Cheese Puff Pie with Shrimp or
   Mushrooms
Challah
Melon Slices with Lemon
Black Tea

Japanese Fresh Blanched Vegetables
Boiled Rice
Jerusalem Artichokes, Mushrooms and
   Spinach with Plum Sauce
Stir-Fried Tofu and Broccoli Spears
Nutmilk and Apples
Green Tea

Italian Fried Cheese Sandwiches with
  Piquant Tomato Sauce
Braised Chard and Almonds
Yeasted Golden Pumpkin Raisin Bread
Cinnamon-Orange Tea

Cream of Fresh Tomato Soup
Artichokes with Sesame Dressing
Avocado Noodles
Cheese Puffs
Oranges, Pineapple and Grapefruit Salad
Iced Jamaica Tea

Tossed Green Salad with Cauliflower
  Fried in Coconut Batter
Sour Cream Dressing
Zhivetch
Hiker's Rye
Peach Lassi
Chamomile Tea

Vietnamese Salad
Dinner Rice Balls
Green Tea

Dinner

Fresh Basil Soup
Tomatoes Stuffed with Fresh Corn
Spinach Lasagne with Cream Sauce
Toasted Challah
Rhubarb Tart
Lemon Grass Tea

Cream of Spinach Soup
Green Salad with Tomatoes
Herb Quiche
Walnut Hearthbread
Cream Cheese
Darjeeling Tea

Bean Sprout and Jerusalem
  Artichoke Salad
Four Seasons Curry
Apple and Raisin Chutney
Dates Stuffed with Cream Cheese
Maté Tea

Oven Pot Vegetable Broth
Vietnamese Salad
Dinner Rice Balls
Sliced Peaches with Lemon Juice
  and Sherry
Green Tea

Tabouleh and Tomato Salad with
    Garbanzos
Greek Onion Pie
Braised Chard with Almonds
Fruit Salad
Coconut Cookies
Peppermint Tea

Iced Gazpacho
Salad Nicoise
Zucchini Stuffed with Cream
Chard Fritatta
Date and Beet Cake
Lemon Grass Tea

Nasturtium and Plum Salad
    with Honey-Lime Dressing
Mexican Corn Pancakes with Chiles and
    Cheese Sauce
Zucchini and Walnuts
Dessert Rice Balls
Bancha Twig Tea

Green Salad with Croutons
Cream of Mushroom Soup
Eggplant Jack
Spaghetti with Green Sauce
Garlic French Bread
Fresh Strawberry Tart
Black Tea

Boiled Brown Rice
Ginger Broccoli
Pepper Date Winter Squash
Green Beans, Sprouts, and Mushrooms in
    Szechuan Black Bean Sauce
Chilled Fruit
Oolong Tea

Indo Chinese Avocado Salad
Bulgur Pilaf
Vegetables Mediterranean
Yogurt and Apricot Pie
Chamomile Tea

Green Salad with Fruit and Honey Lime
    Dressing
Jack and Pepper Enchiladas
Burrito Casserole
Aguacata Picante
Tortillas
Melon
Maté Tea

Tukpa
Moh Moh
Green Beans Szechuanese
Oriental Spiced Cabbage Pickle
Khaptse
Chinese Almond Custard
Tibetan Tea

When our senses are awake it is possible to recognize the vital and transitory *essences* in real foods. These essences may be clearest to us in liquids at times when we aren't distracted by texture, chewing, or thinking. Something in the flavor bespeaks a vital unity. Essential spirits, like the finest wines and brandies, may be the culmination of a long process of preparation, or may be apprehended immediately, as when squeezing an orange. In both cases the true quality of wine or the juice is there as a grace.

The essences of grains and vegetables can also be revealed in a soup. Leftovers seasoned in hot water or fancy soups with overlays of expensive ingredients can be alive, or dead, depending on whether the cook has opened up his senses. The cook's work is in developing the attention and patience to observe (and taste) what is happening in the cooking process. There is art in recognizing when the process is at its peak. A good soup chef knows when to stop.

The best soup stocks are cooked very slowly—at a bare simmer or less. This allows the flavoring to dissolve slowly and enrich the broth rather than to boil and condense to the bottom. Try the Chinese oven-pot method. You can also use the top of the stove—but remember to keep the heat quite low and to allow several hours. Saving the liquid from boiled vegetables can also eventually make a good broth, but the best broths are simmered slowly from fresh vegetables especially chosen for the soup.

One of the simplest and most rewarding soups to make is the gazpacho. Please experiment. Add one vegetable or fruit at a time and taste as you go.

The lentil soup is a simple classic. None of these soups are difficult and all are open to improvisation. There are three "patterns" included in this section that can be followed for making soups from almost any vegetable imaginable.

Gazpachos

After the first exciting harvests of our tomatoes have been fully appreciated, we begin to serve gazpachos. Ice cold and always varied, subtle and shocking, we are awakened at noon with this liquid quintessence. This is one of the most vitamin-rich soups possible, and it is an excellent soup for the cook to prepare in order to train himself to recognize the essences in food. The only "cooking" involved in a gazpacho is what the cook does with his senses.

The traditional gazpacho consists of fresh tomatoes to which green peppers, garlic, onions, cucumbers, fresh herbs, oil, and lemon juice are added. This combination can be blended, mashed, or finely chopped to become anything from a juice to a salad. Most often we blend our ingredients together with ice to form a thick juice and then add diced vegetables for contrasts of flavor and texture.

When making gazpachos, give yourself plenty of time. Wash your vegetables carefully and chop them before blending. Let yourself taste each thing before you blend it and after you combine it with what has gone before. Open your senses. Relax. If you have a blender you can try an interesting gazpacho of oranges, tomatoes, onions, and basil. Make a gazpacho using tomatoes, fresh green peas, cucumbers, onion, and mint. Supplement with radishes and sprouts, jalapenos, green peppers, pineapple, celery, apples and pears. You can add lemon rind, vinegar, miso, nutbutters, nutritional yeast, cooked and raw eggs. The combinations are endless and the results are immediately appreciated.

Gazpachos are never cooked since their virtue lies in freshness. They can be stored in the freezer or refrigerator until quite cold. Or you can blend ice into them. You will find that their flavor changes the longer they sit. They begin to ferment almost immediately. We have had some excellent champagne-like gazpachos that sat in the refrigerator overnight. However, the gazpacho is usually best served as soon as possible. If you ever have leftover gazpacho check it during refrigeration for you may be on your way to vegetable wine. If leftover gazpacho does not contain too much acid, it can be used as a base for a sauce or hot vegetable soup. Really thick and spicy gazpacho is a superb salad dressing.

Iced Gazpacho

9 *rather large ripe tomatoes,*
   diced
1 *or 2 green bell peppers, seeded*
   and diced
1 *medium sweet onion, peeled*
   and diced
2 *cucumbers, peeled and diced*
¼ *cup olive oil, or more to*
   taste
3 *Tbsp. lemon or lime juice*
6 *ice cubes, crushed*
1 *large clove garlic, minced*
¼ *cup fresh basil, minced*
2 *Tbsp. parsley, minced*
salt and cayenne to taste
2 *Tbsp. wine* (*optional*)

Wash and dice the vegetables. Add a few of them at a time to the blender and purée, tasting the emerging gazpacho between each addition. When the vegetables and onion have been blended, add the olive oil and the crushed ice and blend. Add only half of each seasoning, taste, and add the rest of the seasoning to suit yourself.

The gazpacho can be garnished with thinly sliced vegetables, basil, or citrus fruit. Mayonnaise, yogurt, or sour cream can be used either as a garnish or a cup of any one of these may be blended into the soup at the last moment before serving. Serve ice cold. *Serves 4 to 6*

Chinese Vegetable Broth

We call this recipe and the French soup recipe that follows a "pattern" because once you understand the method, you can make distinctive soups from any vegetables on hand. This Chinese soup will be refreshing if the stock is delicately flavored and seasoned with a light hand.

4 *cups Oven-Pot Broth* (*see page 25*) *or homemade soup stock*
1½ *Tbsp. dried mushrooms or ¼ cup fresh mushrooms*
4 *tsp. oil*
1 *clove minced garlic*
½ *tsp. grated fresh ginger*
1 *to 1½ cups thinly sliced vegetables: spinach, zucchini, cucumber, snow peas and water chesnuts, etc.*
4 *tsp., total, light tamari and/or miso*
about 2 tsp. flavoring ingredient: Szechuan black bean sauce (*see page 125*), *oyster sauce, tomato paste, bonito flakes, gomashio, nutritional yeast, etc.*
salt to taste
pepper to taste: black, crushed chiles, Szechuan, etc.
2 *Tbsp.* (*or less*) *dry sherry*
1 *tsp. aromatic sesame oil*

Heat the broth. Sauté the fresh or soaked dried mushrooms in the oil with the garlic, ginger and sliced vegetable for a few minutes or until the vegetable is barely wilted (spinach, chard) or partially cooked (zucchini). Add to the broth. Season to taste. If you want to add noodles, cook them in the broth as you chop the vegetable. If they are the type that get soggy, take them out and add them again, just after seasoning the broth. Garnish with just a little of any or all of the following: finely chopped chives or green onion, finely chopped tomato, finely chopped bell peppers, finely chopped cilantro (Chinese parsley) or shrimp, etc. *Serves 3 to 5*

Egg-Flower Soup

Prepare the recipe opposite without the additional vegetable, season lightly and barely bring to a simmer. Beat one egg and pour it into the broth in a *tiny* stream over the tines of a fork as you move the fork slowly back and forth across the surface of the broth. Add the sesame oil and garnish.

Fresh Basil Soup

In its dried form, basil has such a poor and distorted flavor that it is usually best omitted from any recipe. But fresh basil—there is no other herb to compare with it! If you are fortunate enough to grow it or can purchase it at a rare produce market, then this recipe is yours. Here is a sprightly, savory soup that will wake up more than just your appetite.

⅓ *cup minced and closely packed*
     fresh basil leaves
½ *tsp. tarragon (optional)*
one small clove garlic, minced
3 *Tbsp. butter*
2 *cups chicken broth, V-8, or*
     stock
2 *cups tomato juice*
salt and freshly ground black
     pepper or Tabasco
¼ *cup minced basil leaves*
3 *egg yolks*

Chop the basil very finely in a ½ quart serving bowl. Transfer the basil, tarragon and garlic to a saucepan, and sauté for a few minutes over low heat, then pour the boiling tomato juice and chicken broth over it. Simmer very gently for 10 minutes. Salt and pepper to taste. Beat the yolks in the serving bowl and pour the soup into them, lightly beating with a wire whisk. Have ready ¼ cup or more minced basil to garnish—just how much will depend on your basil's strength. Serve at once. If you are a dill lover, try this with dill, but use quite a bit less of it than the basil this recipe calls for, and add 3 Tbsp. chopped mint. *Serves* 3 or 4

Iced Yogurt Soup

This soup is best if you can prepare it a few days ahead of time. Keep it in a cold refrigerator. An hour or more before serving, put the soup in the freezer to become icy.

1 *large cucumber or zucchini*
3 *cups yogurt or buttermilk*
½ *cup walnuts and/or*
    mushrooms
1 *large clove garlic*
¾ *tsp. salt*
¼ *tsp. freshly ground pepper*
1 *Tbsp. dill weed or more to*
    taste
4 *Tbsp. oil*
1 *small cucumber*
dill weed, to garnish

Dice and seed the cucumber, peeling it if you wish. Put all the ingredients in a blender and purée well. Refrigerate. Put it in the freezer an hour before serving. Garnish each bowl with paper thin slices of fresh cucumber or zucchini and more dill. You may wish to vary the seasonings. Try, for a change, 4 to 8 dried juniper berries blended with ¼ cup of wine, ¼ tsp. thyme and a dash of cayenne. Serve cold with a dollop of sour cream in each cup. This soup is also good with dried or fresh mint, or try a little curry. *Serves* 4

Beer Soup

4 *Tbsp. butter*
4 *Tbsp. flour*
4 *cups rich chicken broth or*
    vegetable stock
2 *cups beer*
½ *tsp. thyme*
¼ *tsp. sage*
½ *tsp. nutmeg*
½ *cup heavy cream*
watercress, croutons (*optional*)

Prepare a *roux* with the butter and flour and then add the chicken broth and beer. Season and simmer for 10 minutes or longer. Add the cream, heat once again and serve. Garnish with watercress and croutons. *Serves* 4 to 6

Avocado Avgolemono

A delicious and distinctive avocado soup probably best described as avgolemono because of the importance of the lemon in its delicate flavor.

4 *cups hearty vegetable broth or*
    chicken stock
1 *Tbsp. grated onion*
2 *tsp. minced parsley*
1 *tsp. minced cilantro* (*optional*)
⅛ *tsp. minced garlic*
1 *tsp. cumin*
½ *tsp thyme*
2 *Tbsp. dry sherry, or more to*
    taste
1 *Tbsp. lemon juice, or more to*
    taste
1½ *or more large ripe avocados*
½ *to 1 cup heavy cream* (*or thick*
    white sauce)

Heat the broth and add the seasonings. Peel and chop one avocado and purée with the hot broth. Return the broth to a saucepan with the cream and heat again, but do not boil. Garnish with more avocado and serve immediately. *Serves* 4 or 5

Cream of Fresh Corn Soup

This easy process can produce anything from a cream corn to a chowder. When the corn is fresh, the soup is beautifully sweet, rich, and simple.

4–6 *ears corn*
½ *cup diced potato*
½ *cup diced onion*
2 *Tbsp. butter*
1½ *cups water*
1 *cup milk, cream, or half and half*
¼ *tsp. cumin*
salt and black pepper to taste

Grate corn from the cob over a bowl to equal 3 cups. This will take from 4 to 6 ears, depending on their size. Peel and dice the potato into small pieces. Dice the onion. Sauté the onion in the butter until it is translucent, then add the water and the potato. When the potato is nearly tender, add only *one* cup of the grated corn. Cook the soup 10 minutes longer. Place the remaining 2 cups of corn in a blender with the milk and purée until very smooth. Add the corn purée to the soup and season to taste. Serve as soon as the soup is hot. *Serves* 4 to 6

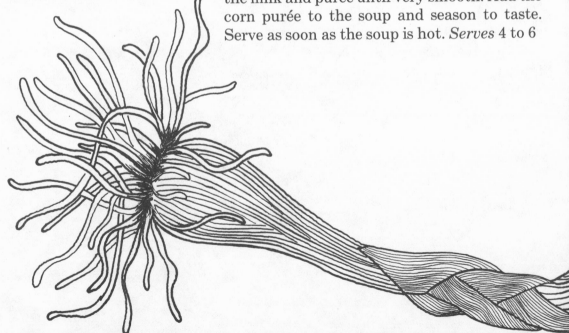

Cream of Spinach Soup

This cream soup pattern recipe works well with any green vegetable. Try fresh or frozen peas and thyme. It's also good with scallop squash, green beans, romaine lettuce, cauliflower, nasturtium leaves, watercress or parsley. Whatever the vegetable, don't overcook it. It should have a healthy vivid color when added to the soup. And never let the soup boil.

½ *lb. fresh spinach or* 1 *cup frozen spinach*
5 *cups milk, soy milk, or part vegetable stock*
4 *Tbsp. butter*
2 *tsp. grated onion*
3 *Tbsp. flour*
1 *tsp. or less salt*
pinch of cayenne
1 *Tbsp. minced parsley*
¼ *tsp. freshly grated nutmeg*
3 *Tbsp. white wine* (*optional*)

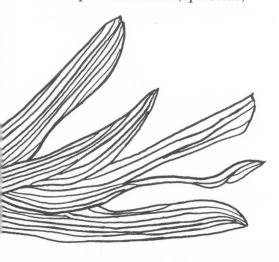

Wash the spinach thoroughly and coarsely chop. Place it in a pot while still wet, cover with a lid and cook it carefully until just wilted. If you use frozen spinach, just defrost it. Put the spinach in a blender with one cup hot milk or stock and purée until quite smooth. Set aside. Add the butter to a soup pan and when melted add the minced onion. When the onion has become transparent, add the flour and stir for a minute over low heat. Add 3 cups milk to the flour-butter *roux* and stir with a wire whisk. When it has become thick (nearly boiling) add the seasonings and the blended spinach. Heat it but don't let it boil. Add the wine, let it mellow for a few minutes and serve.

If you like, you can blend in sour cream before serving, or you may purée the spinach with a cup of yogurt. Soy milk can be used with any creamed soup along with the addition of a little extra butter or oil. *Serves* 4 to 6

French Single Vegetable Soup Pattern

When you perfect this method, you can make a really delicious soup from any vegetable, even rutabagas and parsnips.

3 *cups shredded or diced*
    vegetable (cabbage, green
    beans, peas, squash,
    eggplant, green peppers, or
    mushrooms)
4 *Tbsp. butter*
½ *cup minced onions*
4 *cups vegetable or chicken stock*
spices (cayenne, black pepper,
    thyme, nutmeg, oregano,
    rosemary, etc.)
1 *cup flavorful thickener (tomato*
    sauce, cream sauce, or heavy
    cream)
2 *egg yolks*

Sauté the shredded vegetable in butter with the onion until the onion is transparent and the vegetable is tender. Purée only two cups of the sautéed vegetable with the stock and return to the saucepan with the remaining sautéed vegetable. Bring to a boil and simmer for a few minutes. Season to taste and add tomato sauce, cream, or thick cream sauce and then add the beaten egg yolks. Barely simmer for 5 minutes longer. Garnish with grated cheese or parsley, and serve hot. *Serves* 6 to 8

Basic Vegetable Broth

Every time you steam or boil vegetables or pasta, save the stock. You can keep using this same stock for cooking many vegetables until you have a wonderful broth. This broth will keep indefinitely if it is refrigerated and brought to a boil about three times in every two week period.

To enhance the broth, supplement it with potato skins and the tough ends of vegetables, lifting them out after they have simmered for 30 minutes to an hour. When the broth is rich enough to serve, season it lightly and combine with a few fresh vegetables, green onions, rice, potatoes, or pasta.

Oven-Pot Vegetable Broth

This is an adaptation of a Chinese method of making a vegetable soup stock which is delightfully subtle and quite nutritious. The oven simmering process is useful when you need the burner tops—or if you just want to leave the kitchen for a while. Of course you can cook this stock on top of the stove too. Adapted from Kenneth Lo.

1½ *cups yellow split peas, navy beans, soy grits, dried limas, or other pre-soaked beans.*
½ *cup cashews or raw peanuts*
1½ *cups mushrooms—use older ones that are completely open. Dried mushrooms will improve the flavor.*
2 *to 4 cups coarsely chopped vegetables—choose two or three of the following: carrots, onions, turnips, broccoli stems, cauliflower, cabbage stems and hearts, celery, zucchini, sprouts, etc.*
7 *to 9 cups boiling water.*

Wash and pre-soak the beans, if you have time. Chop the vegetables and combine all the ingreiendts in a heavy Dutch oven or iron pot with a lid. Place in the oven at 325°. Check and stir 15 minutes later. Adjust the oven temperature so that the pot just barely simmers. Cook for 2 more hours. Partially cool and strain through a colander, then through a cheesecloth if you want a clearer broth. Wring the vegetables in the cheesecloth to extract the broth.

You may want to prepare larger quantities to refrigerate for future use. See page 57 for a recipe using the vegetables from the oven-pot. *Yields* 6 to 7 cups

Soups from Dried Beans

These classic soups can be a staple in vegetarian cooking. The dried pea and bean is very receptive to other vegetables and varied seasonings. We feel, however, that the best of these soups use very few ingredients and combined to point out the unique flavor of the bean itself. Here are two of our favorites.

Black Bean Soup

Black beans make a wonderful soup. Depending on the flavorings you use it can even taste like chocolate. If you thin it and season lightly, it will taste something like a good dark miso. We season it many ways, but like it best when it tastes like black beans.

1¼ *cup black beans*
3 *cups water*
¼ *Tbsp. chopped onions or*
    1½ *tsp. or more tarragon*
salt to taste
cayenne to taste
¼ *cup sherry or red wine*

Wash, soak, and cook the black beans until they fall apart. Sauté the onion or garlic in the oil until transparent. Mash and put the beans through a sieve, or purée them in a blender with a little more water. Add the onion, oil, and tarragon. Return to the pan over a low flame. You may need to add a little more water, but the soup should be rather thick. Add salt and pepper to taste. Add the sherry and simmer only a few minutes more.

There seem to be two kinds of black beans: one flavorful and one rather dull. If your black beans are the dull kind—the soup may require more wine, and probably tamari. *Serves* 2 to 4

Lentil Soup

1 *cup lentils*
3½ *cups water*
½ *cup tomato sauce or to taste*
salt
1 *or more tsp. oregano to taste*
5 *cloves garlic or to taste*
lots of freshly ground pepper or
      cayenne
½ *cup tomato sauce or*
      to taste

This is easy to prepare. Wash the lentils, place in your soup pot with the water and soak overnight. If you're short on time, bring the lentils to a boil, turn them off and let them sit 30 minutes. Simmer the lentils until tender and just beginning to fall apart. Add the tomato sauce, more water if necessary, and salt to taste. Add the oregano and finely minced or pressed garlic. Let the soup simmer 3 more minutes. Top with lots of fresh ground pepper or cayenne and serve. This soup is best without too strong of a tomato flavor. The garlic is obviously present, but somehow it all tastes like lentils. *Serves* 2 to 4

Salads

There are people who love salads and people who do not. There are also people who rarely prepare salads for themselves but who do appreciate them when they are made by someone else. These recipes are for people who do not find the traditional green salad very interesting. Each of them has a distinct personality and some of them will surprise you.

When a salad is cold and crisp, it can be an excellent stimulant to the appetite. Some of these salads are also perfect choices to serve at the end of a meal because they can be so much more refreshing than a dessert. There are other salads in this section hearty enough to be the central focus of a meal.

Salads are wide open to creativity. Remember that any food is fair game for the salad-maker. Taste raw fruits and vegetables as you cut them and you will find the size and texture that brings out their best flavor. It may be that the highest honor we can pay a fruit or vegetable is to include it in a salad, so be sure to choose your ingredients for their quality and freshness.

Fresh Spinach Salad with Sesame Dressing

This is one of our favorite salads. We vary the accompanying ingredients but two essential parts remain the same: spinach and a sesame dressing.

The Salad
½ *pound* (6 *cups*) *torn and packed fresh spinach*
½ *cup slightly green pear sliced* (*optional*)
¼ *cup minced sweet onion* (*optional*)
½ *cup chopped or sliced tomatoes* (*optional*)
¼ *cup finely sliced celery* (*optional*)
1 *or* 2 *hard boiled eggs, sliced or crumbled for garnishing*

Sesame Dressing
¼ *cup mild oil*
3 *Tbsp. light tamari*
3 *Tbsp. lemon juice, wine or tarragon vinegar*
¼ *tsp. honey*
½ *tsp. grated fresh ginger*
⅛ *tsp. freshly ground black pepper*
salt to taste
3 *Tbsp. toasted sesame seeds*

Combine the liquid ingredients and season them. Put the sesame seeds in a small skillet over medium low heat and toss or shake them, like you do popcorn, until they are fragrant and light golden brown. Combine with the dressing and serve over the salad. *Serves* 4 to 6

Pressed Cabbage Salad with Skillet Sauce

A new look at salad—if you like this method of preparation you can probably think of many excellent variations.

4 *cups Chinese (Nappa) cabbage*
1 *cup radishes*
1 *cup thinly sliced cucumber*
2 *Tbsp. salt*
1 *cup cold water*
1 *onion*
2 *small chiles, washed and seeded*
4 *Tbsp. oil*
2 *tsp. dry sherry*
1 *Tbsp. aromatic sesame oil (to taste)*
1 *Tbsp. chopped fresh cilantro (to taste) or green onion, minced*

Wash the cabbage and cut the leaves into squares between one and two inches to a side. Slice the radishes and the cucumber very thinly into bite-sized pieces. Mix the vegetables together with the salt in a flat bowl. Put a plate over the top to press the vegetables together and weight it down with a stone or a pan of water. Let the vegetables marinate in the salt for about 3 to 5 hours. Pour a cup of cold water over the vegetables and toss them slightly. Taste them, and if they are still too salty, rinse them with another half-cup of water. Put them in a colander to drain and then gently pat them dry. Chop the onion and seeded chiles. Sauté them in the oil for 5 minutes. Discard the onions and the chiles, pressing the oil from them into the skillet. Add the sherry and the aromatic sesame oil. Toss the vegetables in the skillet sauce and turn them out on a serving platter. Garnish with the chopped cilantro or minced green onion, add tomato wedges, if you wish. Serve hot, at room temperature or chill slightly. *Serves* 6 to 10

Vietnamese Salad

Dishes like this are prepared often in Southeast Asia, but for us the whole experience may be new. This is a festive main dish with wonderful vegetables and an exotic coconut dressing. Traditionally this salad is tossed and served warm, but we enjoy carefully arranging the ingredients on a platter and chilling it well before bringing it to the table.

3 *ounces cellophane noodles*
   (*bean thread*)
1½ *cups barely cooked green*
   peas and/or snow peas
1 *cup diced tomatoes*
¼ *to* ½ *pound bean sprouts*
½ *cup sliced celery*
½ *cup sliced bamboo shoots,*
   Jerusalem artichokes, water
   chestnuts
½ *cup lightly sautéed or raw*
   sliced mushrooms
1½ *cups cooked shrimp*
1 *Tbsp. minced fresh cilantro*
   (*optional*)
1 *slightly green banana, cubed*
¼ *cup crushed roasted peanuts*
¼ *cup toasted dried coconut*
1 *recipe Vietnamese Cold*
   Vegetable Dressing
   (*see page 133*)

Soak the noodles in warm water for 15 minutes or until soft and then boil them in salted water 3 or 4 minutes, cool, and chop into 3 inch lengths. Reserve portions of a few of the ingredients and the toasted coconut for garnishing. Toss the noodles and vegetables, fruit, and shrimp together and toss again lightly with half of the dressing. Arrange the salad on a platter and garnish to suit your fancy. Serve with a little extra dressing on the side. This salad is fun to eat with chopsticks. *Serves 4 to 6.*

Spinach Salad with Feta

Light, yet substantial. Sophisticated and simple. With melba toast and tea, a beautiful and refreshing lunch.

The Salad
2 *bunches fresh spinach* (6–8 *cups chopped*)
¼ *pound feta cheese, crumbled*
3 *Tbsp. minced onion*
¾ *cup cooked black beans*
½ *cup croutons* (*optional*)

The Dressing
½ *cup olive oil*
3 *Tbsp. red wine vinegar*
3 *Tbsp. lemon juice*
1½ *tsp. tarragon*
1 *tsp. tamari*
1 *clove garlic, minced*
salt and pepper.

Carefully sever the spinach leaves and stalks from the heart and soak them in a tub of cold water. Lift the leaves a few at a time from the tub and rinse them under running water. Drain the leaves and pat them dry. Chop the leaves coarsely and chop the stems into small pieces. Put the spinach in a large salad bowl and toss with the onions, half the crumbled feta and half the beans. Arrange the rest of the feta and beans on top and sprinkle on the dressing. Garnish with croutons. *Serves 5*

Indo-Chinese Avocado Salad

The Salad
3 *ripe avocados*
1 *small pink grapefruit*
1 *cup bean sprouts*
½ *cup diced fresh Jerusalem*
   artichokes, or sliced water
   chestnuts, or sliced
   jicama root
½ *cup tender peas*
¼ *cup sliced green onions*
½ *cup slivered toasted almonds*

Coconut-Grapefruit sauce:
⅓ *cup unsweetened dried coconut*
¼ *cup lime juice*
1¼ *cup grapefruit juice*
   (*a little diluted*)
1 *small clove garlic*
1 *tsp. minced fresh ginger*
1 *tsp. honey* (*to taste*)
1½ *tsp. salt*
cayenne or crushed red peppers
   (*to taste*)
3 *Tbsp. fresh basil or cilantro*
   (*optional*)

For the dressing, place in a blender and purée the coconut, lime juice, grapefruit juice, garlic, ginger, honey, salt, cayenne, and basil until smooth. Peel, quarter, and slice the avocados. Section the grapefruit and cut each section in half. Dice the artichokes (or chestnuts or jicama root). Combine all with the peas, onions, and almonds. *Serves 4*

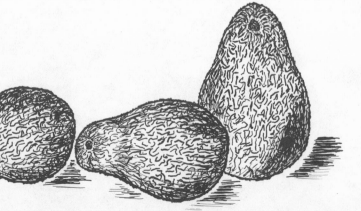

Japanese Fresh Blanched Vegetables

This salad is quickly prepared and perfect for a leisurely and elegant meal. Blanching is a process of dipping food into boiling water for a short time to tenderize and inhibit further ripening. Try using a small wire basket, strainer, or colander that just fits into the pot of water.

Select one or two vegetables from each of the following 3 categories, cut them into thin and beautiful shapes, and place them in separate bowls.

Long blanching (2½ to 4 minutes): carrots, beets, rutabagas, turnips, sweet potatoes, jicama or Jerusalem artichokes

Medium blanching (1½ to 2½ minutes): sliced green beans, Chinese cabbage, radishes, daikon, celery

Short blanching (30 seconds to 1 minute): spinach, chard, mustard greens, watercress

Begin by adding the long blanching vegetables to rapidly boiling water. About a minute later, add the medium blanching vegetables. Two minutes later add the short blanching vegetables. Thirty seconds later, remove the basket of vegetables, rinse them under cold running water, and drain. Be sure to use a pot with quite a lot of boiling water to blanch these vegetables, or the water will cool down so much between additions that the vegetables will lose their flavor and color.

Serve the vegetables with Sesame Dressing (page 30). The vegetables may also be marinated for 10 minutes in this dressing before they are served.

Part of this salad's appeal is in its arrangement. Group the vegetables according to their kind on a large platter. The Japanese do this with such care that the eye enjoys the subtle tastes as much as the tongue.

Salad Nicoise

This delicious salad can either be served as the central dish or served in small portions to introduce almost any meal.

The Salad
2 cups cooked rice
1 small can anchovies, drained and chopped
1 can tuna or ½ cup freshly cooked fish (optional) or 2 Tbsp. capers
2 hard-boiled eggs, chopped
½ cup sliced olives (green or black)
¼ cup chopped green or red bell peppers
¼ cup finely chopped chives or green onions
¼ cup chopped parsley
½ cup diced tomatoes

Dressing Niçoise
½ cup olive oil
¼ cup red wine vinegar
2 Tbsp. lemon juice
1 tsp. Dijon mustard
3 cloves garlic, minced
1 tsp. fresh oregano or ½ tsp. dried lavender
salt and pepper to taste

Assemble the ingredients for the salad but save some of the olives, tuna, peppers, tomato, and parsley for the garnish. Make the dressing and toss half of it with the salad. Garnish and serve remaining dressing on the side. *Serves 4 to 6*

Bean Sprout and Jerusalem Artichoke Salad

This crisp "salad" is a beautifully textured vegetable dish that can be served with any meal.

The Salad:
½ to 1 *cup thinly sliced and chopped Jerusalem artichokes or water chestnuts*
⅓ *pound bean sprouts*
½ *cup thinly sliced celery*
½ *cup uncooked frozen or barely cooked fresh peas* (optional)
2 *Tbsp. minced green onion*
2 *tsp. grated fresh ginger*

The Dressing:
½ *cup mayonnaise*
1 *Tbsp. tamari* (or to taste)
½ *tsp. cumin*
½ *tsp. turmeric*
2 *tsp. lemon juice*
2 *tsp. light wine or water*
dash of cayenne

Combine the mayonnaise, tamari, cumin, turmeric, lemon juice, wine (or water) and cayenne. Toss together with the salad ingredients and serve very cold. *Serves* 4 to 6

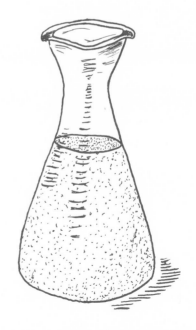

Green Salad with Honey-Lime Dressing

Onions and oranges together? This is traditionally enjoyed in the Middle East and Latin America. The dressing enhances this unusual combination.

The Salad
8 *cups greens: romaine, butter*
    lettuce, red lettuce,
    watercress
2 *oranges*
2 *medium sweet onions*
2 *to 3 avocados*

Honey-Lime Dressing:
⅜ *cup salad oil*
4 *Tbsp. tarragon vinegar*
½ *cup lime juice*
⅓ *cup honey (or to taste)*

For the dressing, combine the oil, vinegar, lime juice and honey and salt to taste. Shred the greens. Peel, quarter, and slice the oranges and avocados. Slice the onions into thin rings. Pour the dressing over the salad and toss it with freshly-ground black pepper. You may garnish with other sliced fruit such as strawberries or plums. *Serves 8*

Nasturtium and Plum Salad

A salad to open the senses. What a first course!

1⅓ *cups shredded fresh*
    unsprayed nasturtium leaves
4 *cups finely shredded Romaine*
1 *cup shredded head lettuce*
1 *cup thinly sliced celery*
8 *sliced Elephant-Heart*
    plums (red)
8 *sliced Kelsey plums* (green)
freshly-ground black pepper

1 recipe Honey-Lime Dressing (see page 38) with an additional teaspoon of tarragon, and a dash of nutmeg. Combine with 2 beaten egg yolks. Garnish with Nasturtium flowers. *Serves 8 to 10*

*These are firm-fleshed plums which are usually crisp and take well to salads, but many other varieties will do.

Tomatoes Stuffed with Fresh Corn

When these vegetables are picked from your garden and prepared immediately, this is a wonderful high-summer delicacy.

3 *medium firm sweet tomatoes*
1 *to 2 ears very fresh sweet corn*
2 *to 3 Tbsp. fresh basil, chopped*
⅓ *cup yogurt cheese (see page 121) or cream cheese*
¼ *tsp. salt*
dash of freshly ground black pepper

Slice off the very top of each tomato and spoon out the interior. Chop the tomato top, combine with the pulp and drain. Grate the corn over a bowl and chop the basil. If you prefer the kernels whole, cut them off the cob with a knife. Combine the tomato pulp, grated corn and corn milk, basil, yogurt cheese, salt, and pepper. Mound the filling in the tomatoes. Don't wait too long to enjoy them. *Serves 3*

Rich Nut Tabouleh

1 *cup bulgur wheat*
⅓ *cup ground roasted sesame seeds*
1 *finely diced and peeled cucumber*
½ *cup finely diced broccoli florets or cauliflower*
1 *cup finely diced fresh mushrooms*
3 *Tbsp. chopped green onions*
¼ *cup minced parsley*
¼ *cup oil*
2 *cloves minced garlic*
6 *Tbsp. lemon juice*
3 *Tbsp. dry sherry*

1 *Tbsp. tamari or more*
½ *cup roasted chopped cashews*
¼ *cup currants (optional)*

Pour boiling water over the bulgur wheat and soak it for 15 to 45 minutes or until soft enough to eat. Drain it thoroughly. Combine with the other ingredients and serve cold. This recipe can also be balanced with the addition of ⅓ cup coarsely ground cooked chick-peas. For an interesting variation, omit the parsley and substitute fresh cilantro or omit the currants and add a tablespoon of grated ginger. *Serves 4 to 6*

Radish and Sour Cream Salad

This is a particularly flavorful combination. It can be a condiment as well as a distinctive salad to begin, or end, a festive meal.

20 *medium red radishes (part*
    may be daikon)
½ *red sweet onion*
½ *tsp. ground caraway and/or*
    1 *tsp. dill leaves*
1 *Tbsp. red wine*
1 *tsp. or more horseradish*
1 *cup sour cream*
1 *tsp. salt*
1 *tsp. honey*

1 *chopped hard-boiled egg*
    (optional)
freshly ground pepper

Wash, trim, and slice the vegetables thinly. Combine the ingredients for the sauce and stir in the radishes. Serve immediately for clear, distinct flavors, or you may refrigerate this salad for an hour or more to increase the subtlety. *Serves* 4

Aguacata Picante (Spiced Avocado)

Try this salad as a small first course, or serve it with a meal as a chutney.

2 *medium onions*
1 *clove garlic*
2 *large green peppers*
2 *small hot red chiles, seeded*
¼ *cup oil*
¼ *cup tomato sauce or paste*
½ *cup lemon juice*
1 *tsp. salt*
3 *or* 4 *large avocados, minced*

Grind the onions, garlic, peppers and chiles through a food mill, *Champion* juicer, or purée them in a blender. Sauté them in the oil until the onions are golden yellow. Add the tomato sauce, lemon juice and salt. Simmer over low heat until done to taste, 5 to 30 minutes. Cool the sauce and gently stir in the minced avocados. Serve cold.

The avocados may also be sliced in thin strips, laid on a bed of lettuce, and covered with the sauce. *Serves* 4 to 8

Tabouleh and Tomato Salad

1 *cup bulgur wheat*
4 *firm tomatoes*
1 *large sweet cucumber*
⅔ *cup fresh parsley or more*
½ *cup green pepper (optional)*
⅓ *cup fresh basil (more or less)*
½ *cup fresh mint (1 Tbsp. mint if fresh basil is used.)*
½ *tsp. oregano*
¼ *cup minced green onion or red onions*
½ *cup olive oil*
⅓ *cup lemon juice*
4 *Tbsp. very dry wine*
1 *tsp. salt*
a little cayenne or freshly ground black pepper
⅓ *cup cooked and coarsely ground chick peas*

Pour boiling water over the bulgur wheat and soak it from 15 to 45 minutes, or until soft but still *al dente*. Drain it well. Chop the tomatoes and cucumber fine and mince the fresh herbs. Mix all the ingredients and correct the seasonings. The chick-peas will provide better nutritional balance if there are no other beans in the meal. This salad is good with a garnish—try olives, for instance. *Serves* 4 to 6

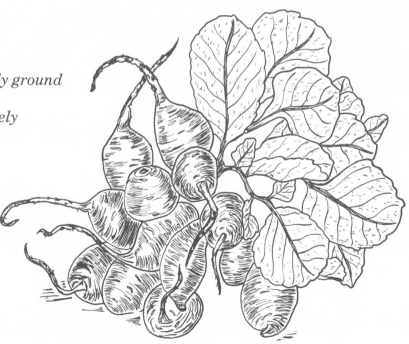

Vegetables

Cooking is gardening—but it's *fast* gardening. Processes of development and maturation that take weeks in the sunshine happen in minutes over the flame. The more you begin to approach cooking vegetables as the continuation of a natural ripening process, the closer you will be to discovering what a vegetable really is.

Most vegetables are not like the grains or dry beans which provide the amino acids to build our requirement of protein. However, fresh tomatoes, chard, or peas do offer us delicate and vital essences, and the value of these probably extend beyond our knowledge of nutrition. To say that each vegetable is a unique *spirit* is to come close to the point.

Most fresh vegetables are best when they are steamed, sautéed, or stir-fried until barely tender and then seasoned or sauced with a very light hand.

In this section we also include a few relatively complex dishes, each dish demonstrating a method of preparation that may be used with many other vegetables as well. Fresh herbs are really vegetables too, and some of these recipes make significant use of them.

Jerusalem Artichokes

There is no other vegetable so badly named and generally misunderstood as this one. This root vegetable is native to America and was cultivated here by the Indians. Early visitors to the colonies took it back to Europe where it was readily accepted, only later to return to the States as an exotic vegetable. It is one of the easiest possible vegetables to grow and thoroughly delicious. Even if you have never tried them before, it would be a wise move to plant the first roots you can buy somewhere in your garden near a sunny fence. The Jerusalem artichoke is really a perennial sunflower and ready to harvest a month after it blooms. You can leave the roots in the ground until after the autumn rains, when they will be sweeter. Wait to harvest the roots until just before using them and they will have clean and tender skins. These roots are said to be one of the only fresh vegetarian sources of pantothenic acid—which is very essential in a diet without meat or dairy products. One of the best ways to use Jerusalem artichokes is to scrub them well and slice them into very thin and small pieces for a salad.

Jerusalem Artichokes with Plum Sauce

This is a very distinctive side dish to serve at an oriental meal. In this recipe Jerusalem artichokes are used as a replacement for water chestnuts or bamboo shoots. You can use them in any Chinese dish that calls for crisp vegetables and the result will be nutritious.

½ *pound spinach*
⅓ *pound Jerusalem artichokes*
½ *pound mushrooms*
3 *Tbsp. minced onion*
3 *Tbsp. oil*

Wash the spinach well, chop coarsely and set aside. Scrub the artichokes and slice them into 1" x ⅛" pieces. Wash and slice the mushrooms and mince the onion. Put the oil in a skillet (that will eventually hold everything) over me-

a small piece of fresh ginger
   (optional)
3 or 4 Tbsp. soy sauce
¼ cup water
4 Tbsp. plum jam or freshly
   mashed plums and honey
2 Tbsp. white wine or water

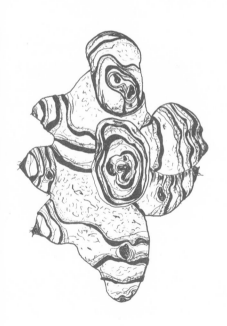

dium high heat and stir a small piece of ginger around until the skillet is hot. Remove the ginger and discard. Add the sliced Jerusalem artichokes and coat well with the oil, stirring until they begin to turn a light gold. Add the soy all at once and stir, coating them well until it has evaporated. Turn the artichokes into a bowl and keep warm. Turn down the heat, add more oil and cook the mushrooms and onions until the onions are transparent. Add the water, plum jam, and the warm artichokes. Stir for a minute and taste the sauce carefully. A secret of Chinese sauces is the sweet/salt balance. The sauce should taste neither sweeter than salty nor saltier than sweet. Correct with either additional salt or plum jam. Turn the heat to high and layer the top of the vegetables with the chopped spinach. Add the wine. Cover the skillet tightly and shift it about a bit as if you were making popcorn. After you have seen steam escaping for about a minute and a half, toss the spinach and vegetables together. The spinach should be almost limp and bright green. Take it off the stove at once and serve. The spinach will continue to cook in the sauce until it cools, so if you like your spinach to have character eat it immediately.

This dish is also delicious with thinly sliced beef that has been lightly sautéed with the onions, set aside and then re-introduced just before serving. *Serves* 4 to 6

Stuffed Artichokes

An elegant and tasty way to prepare artichokes. Prepare them for an occasion when you can take the time to appreciate the contrasting flavors and textures.

4 *large artichokes*
4 *cups bread crumbs or crushed croutons*
⅓ *cup grated Parmesan or other hard cheese*
2 *Tbsp. chopped almonds*
1 *Tbsp. capers or 3 Tbsp. minced olives*
3 *cloves minced garlic*
2 *Tbsp. minced parsley*
salt and pepper to taste
2 *Tbsp. minced basil*
⅓ *cup olive oil*
1 *cup water or stock (¼ cup may be wine)*
grated cheese for garnish (optional)

Remove the outer leaves of the artichokes if they are tough or discolored. Cut the stem so that the chokes can sit upright and trim off ½ inch or more of the tip ends. Wash the artichokes very carefully, spreading the leaves under running water. Tap the artichokes sharply against a sink to loosen the leaves and shake out the water.

Combine the ingredients for the stuffing (from the bread crumbs to the basil.) Starting at the top of the artichoke, pull the leaves slightly away from the core and slip small amounts of the stuffing between the leaves. Continue to stuff the artichoke until you have used up about a quarter of the stuffing. Very gently squeeze the artichoke between your palms to tighten the stuffing. Place the artichokes in a deep saucepan or dutch oven so that they touch each other and the pan. If there is extra room, you can fill the space with a jar. Pour a little oil over each artichoke and add the rest of it to the pan. Add about a cup of water or the stock and wine. Cook them covered over a low heat for about 35 minutes to an hour (depending on their freshness) until they are quite tender. Serve hot. *Serves* 4

Clear-Simmered Chinese Cabbage

This is a classic method of preparing vegetables and it deserves to be better known in this country. The vegetables are gently simmered in a slow oven with a clear broth. They retain their sweet and distinct flavors. Other selections of vegetables can be tried. In any case, the result is simple elegance.

4 *cups Chinese (Nappa) cabbage cut in 1½ inch squares*
⅔ *cup celery, sliced on the diagonal*
¼ *cup mushrooms, sliced*
2 *cups homemade vegetable broth, very lightly seasoned*
1 *tsp. oil*
1 *tsp. salt*
1 *Tbsp. tamari*
black or Szechuan pepper to taste

Preheat the oven to 300°. Wash and cut the vegetables. Strain the homemade vegetable broth through a triple layer of cheesecloth and heat it with the oil. Place the vegetables in a casserole and pour the broth and seasonings over them. Simmer the casserole in the oven for 30 minutes. Turn the oven to 275° and simmer 15 minutes longer. Adjust the seasoning and arrange the vegetables in their casserole or in a clear serving bowl. This is delicious with plain boiled rice. *Serves* 3 to 4

Braised Chard and Almonds

3 *cups chopped and steamed fresh chard*
2 *Tbsp. butter*
1 *clove minced garlic*
½ *cup sliced almonds*
salt and pepper to taste
½ *tsp. chervil, fines herbes, or summer savory*

Melt 2 tablespoons butter in a skillet and lightly sauté a clove of minced garlic with the sliced almonds until both the garlic and almonds are a light golden brown. Toss the warm, drained chard in the skillet with the almonds and add the seasonings. Stir the chard until thoroughly hot and serve immediately. *Serves* 3 or 4

Chard Frittata

Try this one on friends who don't like their chard. Spinach, kale, or mustard green frittata are equally good.

3 *cups coarsely chopped and*
   steamed fresh chard or
   spinach
4 *large eggs*
⅔ *cup breadcrumbs*
½ *cup grated Mozzarella*
   or Jack cheese
salt and freshly ground pepper to
   taste
3 *Tbsp. butter*

Wash, chop, and lightly steam enough chard to make 3 cups (about 6 to 8 cups, raw.) Beat the eggs, add the breadcrumbs, grated cheese, and salt and pepper to taste. Melt 1½ tablespoons of the butter in a skillet and add the chard and egg batter. Disperse the mixture over the pan and let it fry over medium heat, covered, until firm on the bottom. Turn the omelette over and fry it on the other side in a little more butter. Sometimes a little fresh oregano is also good in this. Serve hot. *Serves 4 to 6*

Sweet and Sour Red Cabbage with Apples

1 *head red cabbage*
3 *pippin apples, or any tart*
   apples
1 *onion (optional)*
2 *Tbsp. oil*
½ *tsp. powdered cloves, or more*
1 *tsp. caraway seeds*
1 *Tbsp. or more honey*
3 *Tbsp. vinegar*
¼ *cup chopped prunes or raisins*
salt and pepper to taste

Chop the cabbage a little coarser than for coleslaw. Slice the cored apples, leaving the skin on. Sauté the cabbage and apples. When they are nearly tender, add the seasonings and prunes or raisins. Simmer about 10 minutes longer or until done to your taste. Correct the seasonings and serve. *Serves 3 to 6*

Oven-Fried Eggplant Slices

The key to good eggplant is to cook it quickly. This preserves its texture and flavor. If you like eggplant by itself, this is an excellent method to try.

1 *medium eggplant*
2 *eggs*
2 *Tbsp. tamari*
⅔ *cup or more flour*
⅛ *cup cornmeal*
oil

Preheat the oven to 425°. Cut an eggplant into ½ inch slices. It's a good idea to soak them in salted water for 30 minutes or longer. (Although some people insist that this makes no difference, we have never had bitter eggplant this way.) Drain and pat dry. Beat the eggs and tamari. Fill a wide bowl with ⅔ cup or more flour and ⅛ cup cornmeal. Cover an eggplant slice with the flour, dust the excess flour off, and dip it into the egg; then coat it once again with flour. Put the slices on an edged cookie sheet or skillet lavishly spread with oil. When the sheet is filled with one layer of eggplant, bake at 425° until the bottom is crispy and golden brown (about 15–20 minutes). Check to see if the pan requires more oil, turn the slices over and bake for 8 to 12 minutes more. Good as they are or with a sauce. *Serves* 4

If you like tomato sauce and cheese, see page 76 for Eggplant Jack.

Corn

As the silks burnish to a rusty gold and the first corn begins to ripen in the garden the attention of our community is naturally drawn to the kitchen, and in a wholesome, quite unself-conscious way, the cooks find themselves acknowledged as the principal celebrants of the deep summer ceremony of the corn festival.

Those who have hardly set foot in the area before begin to hang around the kitchen, then around the green piles of corn, and finally enthusiastically begin to do the husking. Maybe the cook just shows them an efficient husking technique and then goes on to prepare the other dishes for the approaching feast. Here's a corn husking method that works efficiently for us:

Husking Fresh Corn

Get a sharp paring knife and cut off the stem end of the ear, exposing the cob and just cutting into the first kernels. Feel the husk at the other end to find where the first large kernels begin and cut there all the way through the cob at that point. You will see the layers of the husk around this end clearly. Take the knife edge and place it next to the kernels, securing the husks next to the blade with your thumb. Pull down. A lot of the husk will come off at once. Just continue to turn the cob and peel with this motion. A good two or three pulls should do the trick.

Roasting Ears

You can roast mature corn but a slightly younger ear will be more tender. Rub the freshly husked corn with soft butter and salt, enclose each ear tightly in foil and put in a 400° oven allowing 20 minutes for a small ear or 30 minutes for a large one. Some people like this especially when enough butter has been rubbed on the kernels that it browns and almost fries the kernels. If you like, pull off the silks, but don't even husk the corn. Just pop them in the oven, bake until tender, and give your friends a chance to enjoy themselves. Do serve with plenty of real butter.

Corn on the Cob

Boiling.   The cook realizes that the huskers are expecting corn-on-the-cob. No matter how many other sensational ways there are to prepare corn, this is the favorite. So the cook readies a large kettle filled with 3 parts boiling water, 1 part milk, salt to taste, and maybe even a small amount of honey. The more cooking liquid the better. As the corn is husked, the last silks are washed off and the ears are put right in the kettle. The kettle is covered and the ears are boiled rapidly until they are tender—from 3 to 8 minutes. The corn is served immediately with butter and salt. The corn water can be refrigerated and used again, or it can become the base for a soup.

Steaming.   Fresh corn is also delicious steamed, as are many other vegetables. If you don't have many ears to cook try this method. You will need a pressure cooker and a folding French steam basket or colander. Put the basket in an inch of boiling water, the ears in the basket, and put on the lid. Let the steam begin to escape from the pressure cooker before you put on the weight. Steaming corn may take up to five minutes longer than boiling, but it leaves many nutrients right in the vegetable. Steam water can be saved for soup, too.

Sweet Corn Essence

This is the way we serve corn to guests from abroad who have never eaten it before. Try fixing it this way as a side condiment when you don't have quite enough corn for everyone. Its also quite good as a spread for toasted eggbread.

Scrape or grate fresh corn into a small pan or into the top of a double boiler. Add butter and heavy cream, perhaps a little honey, and salt to taste. Heat gently, just until barely tender—3 to 4 minutes. Serve hot.

Corn-Patch Spoon Bread

Spoon bread is one of those delectable Southern dishes that relax and nourish at the same time. Fresh corn gives this one a particularly nice flavor and texture.

4 *ears scraped corn*
¾ *cup milk*
3 *Tbsp. butter*
1½ *tsp. salt*
1 *cup yellow cornmeal*
4 *eggs, separated*

Preheat oven to 350°. Wash the corn and scrape off the kernels and corn milk into a bowl. Set aside. Scald the milk and add the butter and salt. Add the cornmeal slowly to the milk while stirring constantly. Return the mixture to the stove and while still stirring, cook for another minute. Add the scraped corn and the beaten egg yolks. (If you use canned or frozen whole-kernel corn, mash it with ¼ cup cream before adding it to the batter.) Beat the egg whites until stiff and fold them into the batter. Pour it into a buttered dish and bake for 30 to 40 minutes. Serve it immediately with fresh butter. This is almost a souffle. You may also wish to try adding ½ cup grated cheese and ¼ cup minced green onions to this batter. *Serves* 4 to 6

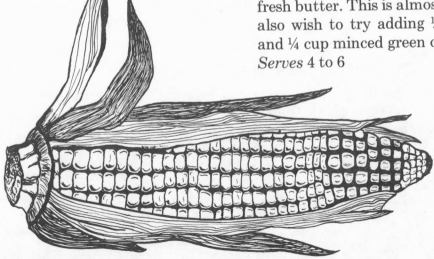

Fresh Corn Souffles

These fluffy little pancakes are a delightful way to serve fresh corn. Delicious either for dinner or breakfast.

3½ cups grated fresh corn
2 beaten egg yolks
½ scant teaspoon salt
1 Tbsp. flour
2 beaten egg whites
butter and oil
maple syrup, fruit purée, or
*   molasses (optional)*

Grate 5 to 7 ears of fresh corn to equal about 3½ cups. Beat the egg yolks and add them to the corn along with the salt. If the corn batter seems a little too runny to fry easily, a little sifted flour will thicken it. Beat the egg whites until stiff and fold them in. Fry the cakes in plenty of butter and oil, turning once, being careful not to overcook them. These are good served plain or with maple syrup or molasses. For a variation, try folding a cup of grated cheese and a little minced onion into the batter before you add the egg whites. *Serves* 2 or 3

Cauliflower in Coconut Batter

1 medium head cauliflower
3 beaten eggs
3 Tbsp. water
1 tsp. flour
½ tsp. salt
⅛ tsp. cayenne
⅓ cup shredded unsweetened
*   coconut*
flour for dredging
oil for frying

Cut the cauliflower into florets about 2½ inches by 1½ inches. Drop them into boiling salted water to cover. Cook them only until *barely* tender, about 4 minutes or less. Drain and rinse in cold water. Pat dry. Make a batter with the eggs, water, flour, salt, cayenne, and coconut. Dredge the florets in flour and then dip them in the batter and deep fry until golden. *Serves* 4 to 8

Ginger Broccoli

This is a savory broccoli dish welcome in an Oriental or Indian meal.

1 *pound fresh broccoli*
1 *medium onion*
1 *firm tomato*

Ginger Sauce
1½ *cups unseasoned vegetable or*
    chicken stock
2 *large cloves garlic*
3 *Tbsp. or more fresh ginger*
1 *tsp. oil*
2 *Tbsp. cornstarch or arrowroot*
½ *cup water*
1 *tsp. salt or tamari to taste*
⅔ *tsp. honey*
cayenne to taste
1½ *tsp. aromatic sesame oil*

Preheat oven to 175°. Cut the broccoli florets into pieces about 1½ inches long and ¾ inch wide. Transfer to a dish. Cut the broccoli stems on the diagonal into ⅛ inch slices and transfer them to a separate dish. Quarter the onion and slice it into pieces ⅛ inch thick. Cut the tomato into wedges and then cut each wedge in half.

To prepare the sauce: heat the broth, then mince the garlic and ginger and sauté in the oil. Combine a cup of the broth with the garlic and ginger, purée in a blender, and then add the purée to the rest of the stock. Simmer 5 minutes. Combine the cold water with the cornstarch and stir into the broth. Season the thickened broth, balancing the "sweet and salt" so that neither flavor dominates the other. Remember when you taste this sauce that it *is* a sauce and not a soup, so all the flavors should be stronger than might seem reasonable. Make sure the fresh ginger taste is very healthy.

To prepare the vegetables you will need a wok, large griddle, or frying pan (just so you also have a large lid to hold in the steam). This method is called steam-frying.

Heat the wok with one Tablespoon oil. Add the cut broccoli *stems* and coat them well with

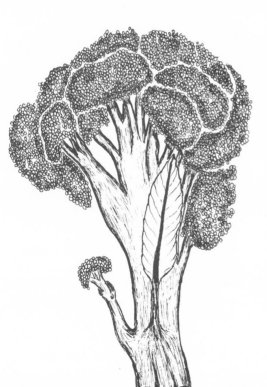

the oil. Toss them in the wok until partially cooked and quite hot—about 3 minutes. Add ¼ cup or less water and clap on the lid. Let them steam for a few minutes and then investigate the wok to see if they need turning or more water. Steam them until just barely tender enough to eat. Transfer them to a large casserole or pan with a cover that is large enough to eventually hold all the ingredients. Keep the broccoli stems warm in the preheated oven.

Steam-fry the onion crescents the same way—don't cook them too long—they should have just a bit of crunch left when they get to the table.

Steam-fry the broccoli florets. Make sure they are crunchy, just tender, and bright green. How much you cook these vegetables depends on how long you intend to hold them before serving. It's better to undercook. You can always sauté them for a minute later.

Add the tomatoes to the wok and let them just heat through, keeping their shape. Assemble all the vegetables, pour the sauce over them and sprinkle on the aromatic sesame oil. Serve hot. *Serves* 4 to 6

Jicama

These look like very large tan-skinned beets, if you ever see one at a produce market. The grocer will usually slice you a piece the size you want to take home. But don't wait to cook it. The skin peels easily if you pull it in strips up from the root-tip. Take a little bite. A little like coconut, a little like a water chestnut. In Mexico, jicama roots are sliced thin and dipped in salt or chili powder and eaten as a snack. They may may also be marinated in lime juice and cayenne. Or dip them like potato chips in spicy cream dressings. Or slice them into fruit salads. We instinctively started using the sliced jicama in oriental cooking. They don't get soggy. In fact, when jicama and Jerusalem artichokes are available, you can forget water chestnuts and bamboo shoots. Sauté sliced jicama pieces with garlic, ginger, tamari and add a bit of aromatic sesame oil before serving. You can sir-fry other vegetables with them too.

Vegetables Mediterranean

2 *cups sliced Jerusalem*
    artichokes or cauliflower
1 *cup sliced mushrooms*
1 *cup sliced celery*
4 *Tbsp. olive oil*
¼ *cup water*
½ *cup green peas*
1 *Tbsp. or more tarragon*
½ *tsp. thyme*
salt and pepper
½ *cup white wine*

Scrub and slice the artichokes into ½ or ¾ inch pieces. Wash and slice the mushrooms. Slice the celery into ¼ inch diagonal pieces. Sauté the mushrooms in olive oil in a small skillet until light brown and set aside. Put the artichokes in a large skillet with olive oil and sauté until barely tender, about 3 minutes. Add a little water (¼ cup), the celery, and the peas. Cover and steam about 5 minutes more. If they are still not quite done add a little more oil and cook slowly without the lid until just tender. Add the herbs, mushrooms with their liquid, and the wine. Heat and serve. This is a great accompaniment for a rich pilaf. *Serves* 4

Oven-Pot Vegetables

Home-Style Chinese food at its simple best. One recipe hot vegetables from the Oven-Pot Broth, (see page 25) unsqueezed, please.

1 *tsp. minced garlic*
1 *tsp. minced fresh ginger, or*
    ½ cup chopped kim chee
    instead of the garlic and
    ginger
½ cup diced onion
½ cup sliced celery, bamboo
    shoots, water chestnuts, or
    Jerusalem artichokes.
1 *Tbsp. oil*
½ cup barely cooked green peas
    or snow peas
tamari and/or miso to taste
1 *tsp. aromatic sesame oil*
¼ cup chopped green onions or
    chives
freshly ground black pepper to
    taste

Sauté the garlic, ginger, onion, and crisp vegetable in the oil for a few minutes and add to the hot but unpressed Oven-Pot Vegetables. Add the hot green peas. Season to taste with the miso or soy sauce and aromatic sesame oil. Garnish with minced green onions. Serve this with steamed brown rice.

An alternative but good spicing for these vegetables is the "3 T's". Add 1 teaspoon ground turmeric, 1 teaspoon tarragon and 1 teaspoon thyme. (Another alternative is to spice with a little garlic, miso, salt and freshly ground black or Szechuan pepper. *Serves 4 to 6*

Curried Peas and Mushrooms in Yogurt

Almost any other vegetable may be substituted for the peas. This is a nourishing and delicious side dish for any meal and can be served hot or cold.

1 *lb. mushrooms*
1 *cup minced sweet onion*
1½ *cups fresh peas (about 1½ lbs. unshelled)*
5 *Tbsp. oil or clarified butter (ghee)*
½ *tsp. black mustard seeds*
1½ *tsp. curry powder*
1 *cup plain yogurt*
1 *tsp. salt*
2 *Tbsp. freshly minced cilantro (Chinese parsley, or green coriander)*

Slice the mushrooms into paper thin pieces, mince the onion, and shell the peas. Set aside. Pour the oil or ghee in a larger skillet and heat. Add the mustard seeds and sauté them for about half a minute. Add the minced onion and stir for about 7 or 8 minutes until transparent. Stir in the curry mixture. Add the yogurt and bring to a boil. Stir in the peas and salt, stirring constantly for about 3 more minutes. Add the mushrooms and half the cilantro, turn the heat very low and simmer for about 15 minutes or until the peas and mushrooms are tender. Garnish with more cilantro. *Serves* 4 or 5

Winter Squash

The hard-shelled squashes are known as winter squash because they will keep after harvesting almost until it is time to plant them again the following spring. We lay up a good store of these and cook them in endlessly varied ways. The squash family also includes pumpkins, and generally, you can substitute one for the other.

When the usual baked, stir-fried, and creamed recipes become tiresome, you can peel and cut winter squash like french fries, coating them with flour or a light batter and deep fry—or try small pieces of tender squash in pancake batters.

Pepper-Date Winter Squash

A South Chinese welcome for an old friend.

2 *cups peeled, seeded, and cubed*
　butternut or banana squash.
　Cut the cubes an inch or a
　half inch to a side.
2 *Tbsp. oil*
1½–2 *tsp. ginger, minced*
1 *large clove garlic, minced*
1 *cup cubed green bell peppers*
8 *dates, seeded and cut in fourths*
1½ *tsp. honey*
⅛ *tsp. crushed dried chile*
　peppers, or to taste
¾ *cup vegetable or chicken broth*
2 *Tbsp. sherry*
2 *tsp. light tamari*
1 *Tbsp. cornstarch or arrowroot*
1 *tsp. aromatic sesame oil*
½ *tsp. ground Szechuan pepper,*
　or freshly ground
　black pepper

Prepare and slice the vegetables. Sauté the squash with the ginger and garlic in the oil over medium heat until nearly tender. If the squash still seems dry and tough, add a little water, cover, and steam a few minutes more. Add the green peppers and sauté 2 minutes. Add the dates, honey, crushed chiles, and toss. Sauté the vegetables another minute, and then remove from the heat and cover.

Prepare a sauce with the stock, sherry, tamari, and cornstarch. Stir until thickened. Pour the sauce over the vegetables and heat. Correct the seasoning. Garnish with a teaspoon of the aromatic sesame oil sprinkled over the top of the dish, and Szechuan pepper. This is an excellent side dish in a Chinese menu. Serve hot. *Serves 4*

Steam-Braised Scallop Squash

A simple recipe that will also gracefully distinguish the delicate flavors and textures of cauliflower, new potatoes, or fresh lima beans.

2 *cups scallop squash*
2 *Tbsp. butter or oil*
water
salt to taste
1 *or* 2 *Tbsp. white wine*
½ *tsp. lemon juice*
½ *tsp. tarragon*
cayenne or black pepper to taste

Wash and cut tender young scallop squash into quarters, like small sections of an orange. Put them in a skillet over medium low flame with a little butter or oil, coating them evenly. Sauté them until partially cooked, having turned a deeper green and becoming slightly transparent. Add just a little water and cover with a lid to steam—about 3 minutes. Take off the heat. Salt to taste and add the white wine and fresh lemon juice. If you like tarragon, add just a little bit, otherwise, they are seasoned enough with a dash of cayenne. This squash is good hot or very cold. If you serve it cold, dust before serving with finely minced parsley—or you may skip the tarragon and season with a little finely chopped mint. *Serves* 2 or 3

Zhivetch with Feta

A savory Romanian vegetable casserole, delicious steaming hot or quite cold. One of the best of the Central European "well-cooked" vegetable dishes.

1 *medium eggplant, peeled and cubed*
2 *small green peppers, sliced into rings*
2 *to* 3 *cups cabbage, coarsely diced*

2 *onions, sliced into rings*
5 *tomatoes, sliced*
½ *lb. or more feta cheese, crumbled*

3 *cups soup stock or more*
½ *cup red wine*
½ *cup olive oil*
3 *Tbsp. caraway seeds*
2 *Tbsp. or more fresh dill*
salt and pepper to taste

Preheat oven to 350°. Wash and slice the vegetables, arranging each kind in its own layer in a 3 quart or larger casserole. Place the feta cheese over 2 layers. Season the soup stock and add the olive oil. Pour the stock over the vegetables, cover, and bake for an hour and 15 minutes, or until quite done. *Serves* 6

Butternut Squash and Cheese Casserole

This is a good breakfast dish. Also good with soup, salad, and bread.

1 *butter-nut squash or other*
    winter squash
1 *egg*
salt and pepper
2 *or* 3 *Tbsp. nutritional yeast*
3 *to* 5 *Tbsp. butter*
½ *cup cubed cheese*

Preheat oven to 325°. Peel the squash, seed, and coarsely chop. Steam it until tender. (If you have no steamer and must boil it, don't let it get mushy. Or, you may use prebaked squash.) Mash the squash well and add a beaten egg, salt and pepper to taste, the nutritional yeast, and the butter. If the squash filling seems too stiff, add a little milk, if too thin, add another egg. Cut your choice of cheese (Colby is good) into ½ inch chunks and fold into the batter. Turn the squash into a small buttered casserole dish. Top with more cheese if you like. Place in a 325° oven and bake until quite hot, about 30 minutes. This casserole is also good if you add a cup of onions that have been sautéed until sweet and dark golden brown. *Serves* 3 or 4

Zucchini

Most people seem to buy or to plant zucchini because it is cheap and easy to grow. Too often a few weeks of its season is enough, and the zucchini remains in the kitchen like a dull houseguest that insists in overstaying his welcome. When it is time for zucchini again, why not reintroduce yourselves? Perhaps because we grow it in a meadow that overlooks the ocean we think of zucchini as a sea-vegetable and we taste its crisp, clear, and "cooling" nature. In fact, we often use it as if it were a "cooking cucumber" and in that way preserve its unique strength. Here are a few recipes for tasting zucchini:

Zucchini and Walnuts

A simple and elegant dish.

zucchini
oil and/or butter
walnuts
salt

Wash young zucchini, and slice them lengthwise in half. Then cut each half into slices like half-moons. Put a little oil in a frying pan and add walnut halves or pieces (about ¼ of the volume of zucchini). Lightly stir the walnuts in the oil with a dash of salt while stirring until they are a little darker and crisper. Remove the walnuts and set them aside. Add a little more oil and butter to the pan and add the zucchini. Stir and toss them lightly until nearly done (still firm but translucent at the edges), combine with the walnuts and salt to taste. Toss a few times and serve quite hot.

Zucchini Stuffed with Cream

This is a Mexican dish, and an excellent way to use cream cheese as well as zucchini. Just reading this recipe to your friends and to your zucchini plants may improve morale and inspire cooperation.

5 *medium zucchini*
water
3 *Tbsp. minced onions*
1 *cup chopped mushrooms*
2 *Tbsp. oil*
½ *tsp. salt*
dash of cayenne
6 *to 8 ounces cream cheese*
¼ *tsp. cumin*
1 *cup sour cream*
2 *or 3 egg yolks*
parsley, chili powder, cherry
    tomatoes for garnishing

Preheat the oven to 325°. Select fresh, firm, medium-sized zucchini (6″ to 8″) and put them in a pan with enough boiling water to cover. Cook them about 10 minutes or until barely tender. Lift them carefully from the pan and let them cool in cold water. Drain, slice them in half lengthwise, and scoop out the seed cavities into a bowl. Sauté the minced onion with the chopped mushrooms in the oil. Drain the mushrooms, saving the juice for a soup, and mix with the seasonings, the scraped zucchini, and the cream cheese. Stuff the zucchini halves with the seasoned cream cheese and mushrooms and put them in an oven-proof serving dish that has been lightly oiled. Combine the sour cream with the yolks. Spread the sour cream over each half and bake about 15 to 20 minutes. Garnish with parsley and a little chili powder. You may also garnish them either before or after baking with a sliced cherry tomato. Try seasoning with a little dill or ground caraway instead of the cumin and chili powder. *Serves* 5 to 8.

Zucchini Boats with Cheese

zucchini
onion
butter
eggs
salt
pepper
oregano, garlic, basil
cheese
cornmeal

Preheat oven to 350°. Parboil whole zucchini in water until just barely tender. Slice the zucchini lengthwise. Scoop out the seeds and pulp leaving about ¼ inch around all sides. Finely chop some onion (to equal about ⅛ of the zucchini pulp) and fry it in butter until nearly transparent. Add the zucchini pulp and cook about 3 minutes longer. Cool the filling slightly and add eggs enough to make a heavy batter (about 1 egg to ¾ cup filling). Salt, pepper and season to taste. Add grated cheese (about ¼ cup to 1 cup filling). Spoon the filling into the boats and top the filling with cornmeal that has been mixed with melted butter. Put the boats in a pan that has short sides and fill with ¼ inch hot water. Bake in the oven for about 40 minutes.

Zucchini can also be stuffed with a mixture of cooked grain and a spicy tomato sauce. Bake them until nearly done, top them with Parmesan and grated Jack cheese and serve them when the cheese bubbles.

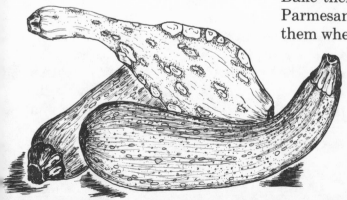

Zucchini Vinaigrette

Zucchini Vinaigrette is representative of many refreshing cold vegetable dishes that can complement the salad as well as the entrée.

3 cups sliced zucchini
⅓ cup wine vinegar
3 Tbsp. lemon juice
2 Tbsp. dried mustard or
*   tarragon*
2 cloves garlic
1 Tbsp. dill
1 cup olive oil
salt and freshly ground pepper

Wash and slice zucchini in ½ inch pieces to make about 3 cups. Pour 3 cups boiling water over the zucchini and let stand about 5 minutes. Drain. Then make the vinaigrette sauce from the vinegar, lemon juice, mustard or tarragon, grated or pressed garlic, dill, olive oil, salt, and pepper. Pour the sauce over the vegetables and refrigerate them overnight or longer. Sliced mushrooms, black olives, green onions, capers and green nasturtium seeds are also very good additions to this dish.

Try this recipe with broccoli or cauliflower florets but drop these vegetables in boiling water for about 3 minutes until just barely tender. Drain and rinse them in cold water to stop the cooking process before you place them in the sauce. Also try other summer squashes, green beans, rutabagas, new potatoes, anise, celery, or peas either singly or in combination. A little curry powder can be substituted for the dried mustard in the sauce and the marinated vegetable served with sour cream or yogurt. *Serves* 5 to 6

Entrees

Here is a selection of main dishes from curries to soufflés. The decision as to what actually constitutes a main dish is a little arbitrary, so you may find what you are looking for under vegetables, pasta, or even soups and salads. The idea of an "entrée" is really left over from the days of roasts and goulashes. A good vegetarian meal doesn't need an "entrée", but there may be one dish just a bit fancier with a little extra cheese or protein that you would like to place in the center of the table.

Four Seasons Curry

This is an example of an entrée that is really a collection of a number of vegetable dishes. You may cook any of your favorite vegetables separately and arrange them at the last moment on a bed of potatoes, pasta, or grains to create a unified and special meal. In this case, three separate curries compose the finished dish.

Here are a few suggestions for other entrées composed from side dishes:

Mediterranean: a large platter of Mediterranean Pilaf (page 102) with a ring of steamed green pepper strips and Cauliflower fried in Coconut Batter (page 53), Falafel (page 94) in the center, and a rich tomato sauce on top.

Milanese: a large platter of wholewheat pasta tossed with a little garlic butter and Parmesan cheese with a ring of Braised Chard and Almonds (page 47) and Steam-Braised Scallop Squash with White Wine (page 60) in the center.

Naturally, there are many other combinations, so just use your imagination. Arranging three or more dishes on a large platter creates a special meal that is more fun to prepare and to eat than the same things when they are served separately.

Part One: Curried Fried Potatoes

This is a delicious way to serve potatoes anytime as well as being the basis for this dinner.

3 *medium large potatoes*
water
butter and/or oil
2 *cloves garlic, minced*
1½ *tsp. cumin*
¾ *tsp. turmeric*
1½ *tsp. paprika or more*
dash of cayenne
salt
fresh minced parsley

Peel the potatoes and slice them for home fries: about ¼ inch thick and 2 inches long by one inch wide. Put them in boiling water and cook them until just barely tender, not done. Take them off the stove immediately and run cold water into the pan to cool the potatoes completely and stop the cooking process. Drain them well and pat dry. Cover the bottom of a large skillet with oil or butter and add the minced garlic and the potatoes. Fry them on each side until they begin to turn golden and nearly crisp. Add the other spices and salt to taste, turning the potatoes until well coated. Continue to fry them until done to your taste. If you are serving these separately, toss minced parsley through them. If you are serving them as part of this dinner put them in a very low (200°) oven until you are ready to assemble all the ingredients.

Part Two: Creamed Curry Sauce

2 *Tbsp. butter*
2 *Tbsp. flour*
¼ *tsp. ginger*
¼ *tsp. cumin*
¼ *tsp. coriander*
¼ *tsp cardamon*
¼ *tsp. turmeric*
½ *tsp. nutmeg*
dash cayenne
salt to taste
2 *cups milk or more*
3 *Tbsp. white wine*

Begin a white sauce by adding the butter and flour to a sauce pan, the spices from ginger through nutmeg. Cook on low heat about 1½ minutes. Turn up the heat a little and add the milk. Stir with a wire whisk until thickened, but not boiling. Add salt and cayenne to taste and adjust the spices. A few minutes before you are ready to pour the sauce over the vegetables (see below) add the wine. You may wish to add only half the indicated amount of spices to this sauce first and then increase any or all of them to suit yourself.

Part Three: Ginger Glazed Carrots

This is a piquant carrot dish best served as a condiment.

1 *cup sliced carrots*
1 *Tbsp. ground or grated fresh*
   ginger or equivalent
   powdered ginger to taste
1 *Tbsp. oil*
2 *Tbsp. brown sugar*
1 *cup water*
1½ *tsp. cornstarch*
2 *Tbsp. tamari*
¼ *tsp. cider vinegar*
   (optional—use for a
   sweet-sour flavor if you wish)
¼ *tsp. ground fennel or star*
   anise

Scrub the carrots and slice them diagonally. Steam, stir fry, or boil the carrots until tender. Have ready the following sauce to cover them: in a saucepan combine the fresh ginger and oil and cook slowly for a minute. Add the brown sugar and caramelize. Carefully add the water mixed with the cornstarch and the tamari. If you would like the sauce slightly sour, add the vinegar. Add the ground fennel or anise. Stir with a wire whisk until clear and pour over the carrots. Let the carrots absorb the flavors a while before serving.

Part Four: Broccoli and Onions

½ *lb. or more broccoli and/or*
   cauliflower
½ *onion*

Cut the broccoli into florets about 1½ to 2 inches wide and 3 inches long. Slice the hard stem end on the diagonal. Slice the onion into strips or chunks. Steam, stir fry, or boil the vegetables until almost done. Drain and cover. The broccoli should be bright green and still crisp, but tender.

Putting It All Together

Garnish
1 *bell pepper*
1 *or* 2 *tomatoes*

Slice a bell pepper into rings and steam, stir fry, or boil until bright green and just tender. Set aside. Cut the tomato into small wedges.

Select a very large serving platter and circle the rim with all the potatoes. Arrange the broccoli florets and onions in a smaller circle inside the potato ring. Ladle the curry sauce inside the broccoli ring, letting the florets show their bright green. Put the ginger carrots in the center of the sauce. Now arrange the pepper slices over the carrots and garnish the edges of the dish with the fresh tomato.

You may want to serve this dinner with a few other condiments, such as coconut, ground peanuts, hard-boiled egg, or chutney, but this curry is quite enough without them. Good with a green or fruit salad and a crisp bread. *Serves* 3 to 6

Frittata

This is a very thick Italian omelette with vegetables. Delicious sliced and served hot or cold with salad and crusty bread. It is traditionally eaten plain, but if you happen to have a little spicy tomato sauce on hand it would be a good compliment to this specialty.

¼ *cup zucchini cut in rounds,*
   then split in half
¼ *cup chopped onions*
½ *cup sliced very small new red*
   potatoes (optional)
½ *cup diced fresh meaty tomato,*
   drained
½ *cup fresh spinach, chopped*
   coarsely (or your choice of
   vegetables)
9 *large eggs, beaten*
½ *cup bread crumbs*
¼ *cup grated Parmesan cheese*
¼ *cup grated Jack cheese or*
   Mozzarella
1 *tsp. salt*
1 *Tbsp. fresh basil and 1 tsp.*
   fresh fennel leaves, or 1 tsp.
   fresh dillweed and ½ tsp.
   fresh thyme
2 *Tbsp. light wine or marsala*
½ *tsp. freshly ground black*
   pepper
4 *Tbsp. butter*

Wash and slice the vegetables. Combine the beaten eggs, breadcrumbs, cheese, and the seasonings. Melt the butter in a small iron skillet and coat the sides well. Sauté the onion and the new potatoes for 2 minutes and then add the other vegetables. Pour the egg mixture over the top and turn the heat to medium low. Press the omelette top to insure good penetration of the vegetables by the eggs. As the omelette cooks, loosen it from the sides of the pan; when the bottom is firm, loosen that also. When the surface is nearly dry, place a lid over the top and turn the omelette upside down on to it. Slide the omelette back into the skillet (it may need a little more melted butter) and lightly brown that side too.

This omelette can also be baked in the oven in a well-buttered flat casserole dish or skillet at 325° for 25 minutes. *Serves 5 to 7*

Mushroom and Herb Quiche

Crust
¾ *cup flour*
⅓ *cup butter*
½ *tsp. oregano*
¼ *tsp. allspice*
¼ *tsp. salt*
4 *Tbsp. cold water*

Filling
¼ *lb. sliced mushrooms*
2 *Tbsp. butter*
2 *Tbsp. grated onion*
1¼ *Tbsp. flour*
2 *Tbsp. dry sherry*
2 *beaten eggs*
¾ *cup milk*
½ *tsp. salt*
⅛ *tsp. white pepper*
¾ *cup grated Jack cheese*
3 *Tbsp. minced parsley*
¼ *cup Parmesan cheese*

Preheat oven to 450°. Combine the flour, salt and spices and cut in the butter. Sprinkle with the cold water, roll it out, and line a 9-inch pie pan with the dough. If the dough ever seems too moist, it may be patted into the pie tin. Bake the crust at 425° for 10 minutes and cool. Or, you may use any recipe for crust.

Sauté the mushrooms in the butter with the onions (reserve 8 slices to decorate the top). Add the flour and sauté 2 minutes longer, while stirring. Take it off the heat and add the sherry. Beat the eggs and add the milk, salt and pepper. Combine the mushrooms with the egg mixture and stir in the Jack cheese and parsley. Dust the bottom of the pie shell with the Parmesan and pour in the filling.

Garnish the top with the extra mushrooms and bake at 450° for 10 minutes. Turn the oven to 350° and bake about 20 minutes longer or until just set. *Serves* 6 to 8

The Souffle Pattern

Here we present the basic structure of any soufflé. A few minutes of studying this pattern will enable you to make any kind of soufflé that may appeal to you. This pattern is based on 1 egg. In order to use it you will need to know the following:

1. A one egg soufflé is a modest serving for one person, 1½ egg soufflé a medium serving, and a 2 egg soufflé is an ample serving as a main dish.

2. Allow one quart of casserole volume for every 2 eggs (although a 3 quart casserole *can* be adequate for an 8 egg soufflé).

So, for instance, to serve 10 very hungry people you might make two 5 egg soufflés in two 2½ quart casserole dishes.

Batter
1 *Tbsp. butter or oil*
1 *Tbsp. flour (white, corn, rice, whole wheat, etc.)*
⅓ *cup liquid (milk, vegetable or meat stock, fruit juice)*
1 *egg*
⅓ *cup flavoring ingredient (cheese, puréed vegetable, fruit)*
¼ *tsp. salt*
¼ *tsp. spices*

Preheat oven to 350°. Make a bechamel sauce by heating the butter or oil and flour. Then add the liquid, stirring until blended and thick. Combine with the egg yolk, flavoring, salt and spices. Leaven by folding in the egg white beaten until stiff but still moist (with or without a pinch of salt and ⅛ teaspoon cream of tartar). Bake in a greased casserole at 350°–375°.

 1 to 4 egg soufflé: about 20 minutes
 4 to 8 egg soufflé: about 45 minutes

For flavoring try minced and sautéed mushrooms or onion; Romano or Parmesan cheese; thyme and Worchestershire; puréed spinach, fontina cheese, cayenne and nutmeg; puréed fish, wine, thyme and tarragon, cayenne, and clam juice; minced strawberries, honey, white wine, and apple juice; puréed dried or fresh apricots, sherry, lemon juice, and honey; etc.

Some soufflés are especially nice served with a light bechamel (white) sauce seasoned with a complimentary flavoring. Dessert soufflés are good with a thickened fruit juice sauce made with a touch of cognac. Sauces are best served in a separate bowl so that your guests may help themselves to as much as they need.

There is the soufflé made with cream cheese, honey, and real vanilla bean juice. Serve it with a light fudge sauce. Or try the soufflé of jalapenos peppers, cheese, mushrooms and black olives, oregano and cumin served with a tomato and anchovy sauce.

Eggplant Jack

This is a very satisfying entrée. Rich, filling, and quite easy to prepare. One of the best eggplant dishes we know.

tomato sauce
spices
Jack cheese
parsley
Parmesan cheese

Prepare the eggplant slices as on page 49, except that just after you turn them over the first time, spoon a rich, medium thick, tomato sauce on top of them. We enjoy a sauce that is sweet and flavorful with garlic, oregano, nutmeg, and lots of powdered cloves. Top the sauce with slices of Jack cheese. Return them to the oven. They are ready to serve when the cheese is melted and bubbly. Garnish with parsley and grated Parmesan. *Serves* 4 to 6

About Enchiladas:

The fillings and sauces for enchiladas are up to you. All you need are tortillas and your imagination. Try:

1. sautéed brown rice, toasted almonds, raisins, spices, cilantro and chopped cooked garbanzos with a little cheese.

2. choose any cut of meat (except hamburger) and combine with cumin, water, crushed chiles, salt, paprika and chopped onions. Boil until nearly dry and use for filling.

3. cooked chicken or fish with cheese, cilantro, gomashio and sautéed celery or Jerusalem artichokes.

4. refried beans, peppers, cheese and olives.

Jack and Pepper Enchiladas

Choose and prepare your sauce (try Salsa Verde, page 129) and then get to work on these enchiladas. Allow yourself plenty of time because they are fun to make. They can be prepared hours ahead, heated with additional sauce and then garnished just before serving.

2 *medium onions, chopped*
2 *small cloves garlic, minced*
butter or oil
salt and cayenne to taste
oil for frying tortillas
12 *corn tortillas*
1½ *cups Red Chili Sauce, or*
    Salsa Verde (see Sauces)
2 *cups chopped bell peppers*
    and/or chopped, peeled and
    seeded jalapeno peppers
grated cheese and/or sour cream
minced green onions for
    garnishing

Sauté the onions and garlic until nearly transparent and add the peppers. Sauté them until tender but still a little crisp. Season to taste and keep warm. Grate the cheese. Pour ½ inch oil into a skillet and heat. Fry each tortilla on each side just until soft and a little puffy. Don't fry them too long or they will be too stiff to roll up with the filling. Dip each softened tortilla into a shallow pan of the sauce you have chosen immediately after it is fried and stack them until all are done.

Combine the onions, peppers, and cheese and place enough in each tortilla to roll into a good, thick enchilada. Place them, folded edge down, in a shallow casserole or oven-proof serving dish that is lightly oiled and sauced. You can cover and refrigerate these enchiladas until later. To bake, first pour more sauce over them and top them with a little grated cheese. Put them in a 325° oven until hot, about 20 minutes. Garnish with sour cream and minced green onions. Serve hot. *Serves* 4 to 6

Sesame-Egg Crepes

These crêpes are delicious with tamari or they can be rolled around sprouts and vegetables with just about any kind of sauce. A nourishing foundation for a quick one-dish meal, whether Chinese, Mexican, or French.

2 *eggs*
dash of tamari or salt
1 *Tbsp. water*
½ *tsp. aromatic sesame oil*
2 *to* 3 *Tbsp. freshly toasted*
    sesame seeds
1 *Tbsp. minced green onion*
    (*optional*)
1 *Tbsp. cooking oil*
an 8-*inch skillet*

For each crêpe, beat the eggs and add the salt water, sesame oil, sesame seeds, and green onion. Pour the cooking oil in a small skillet and tip it to coat the sides. Place the skillet over a low flame and when it is hot (but not so hot that it smokes) carefully pour the batter into the center. The batter will spread over the bottom and touch the sides. Cover the skillet and cook the crêpe very slowly for a few minutes. When the top of the crêpe has almost set, turn off the heat and leave the skillet covered a few minutes longer. When the crêpe is firm, slide it out of the pan and serve it filled or plain, hot or cold. *Serves* 1 or 2

Norwegian Crepes

This batter can also be made the night before and refrigerated. It is very similar to a regular crêpe, is easier to prepare, and offers more protein. Depending on the filling you choose, this pancake can be the star attraction at breakfast, lunch, dinner, or dessert.

4 *eggs*
1 *tsp. salt*

Beat the eggs until very light, add the salt, honey, and beat again. Add the oil, milk, and

1¾ *cups milk and/or cream*
1 *Tbsp. oil or melted butter*
1¼ *cup flour (any variety*
    depending on your choice
    of filling)

sift the flour into the mixture. Stir until well combined. Let the batter sit at least one-half hour or overnight.

Coat the bottom of a large medium-hot skillet or griddle with oil or margarine and pour in enough batter to cover the surface nearly 1/16 of an inch. When the pancake has just cooked through, it can be slid onto a plate and kept in a very low oven until all are prepared. No need to turn it over and fry on the other side. *Serves* 3 to 5

We make crêpes about 8 inches wide and a foot long on a large grill. After the filling is scattered over its surface, the crêpe is rolled up and placed on a serving platter. These can be held in a warm oven for up to 30 minutes, then sauced, garnished, and served hot. They are a favorite, regardless of the filling.

Filling Suggestions: (1) Beaten cream cheese and finely sliced fresh fruit (pineapple, bananas, strawberries). (2) Apple Cider Sauce made with plenty of apples (see page 124). (3) Sour cream, grated cheese, parsley, green onion, and hard-boiled eggs. (4) Stir-fried vegetables. Cover the rolled pancakes with a light white sauce with a sprinkle of cheese on top. These pancakes can be quite elegant for a brunch or supper dish when topped with cheese and warmed in the oven until the cheese just melts. Garnish with watercress and halved cherry tomatoes. *Serves* 4 to 8

Mexican Corn Pancakes with Cheese Sauce

This is a surprising pancake for breakfast. It makes a good brunch or dinner, too.

Pancakes
2 egg yolks
2 Tbsp. melted butter or fat
⅔ cup cream style corn
½ cup or more buttermilk
⅛ cup Parmesan cheese
    (optional)
1 cup yellow cornmeal
1 tsp. baking soda
1 tsp. salt
1 tsp. brown sugar or honey
2 egg whites
¼ cup fresh jalapeno peppers,
    sautéed lightly (or half a
    small can of jalapenos),
    sliced julienne, or fresh sliced
    green pepper, or both.
¼ cup chopped and well drained
    tomatoes (pick a very fine
    meaty tomato for this)
3 Tbsp. finely minced onion

Cheese Sauce
3 Tbsp. butter
3 Tbsp. flour
3 cups milk
1 cup grated cheddar or other
    cheese
dash of cayenne and/or nutmeg

Separate the eggs and set the whites aside. Beat the yolks and add the butter, cream corn, and ⅓ cup buttermilk. Sift the dry ingredients together and combine with the liquid ingredients. If the pancake batter is a little heavy, add more buttermilk. Beat the whites and gently fold into the batter. Lightly fold in the vegetables. Fry as usual in a mixture of half butter and half oil. These are delicate pancakes and require a little extra care when you turn them in the skillet.

For the cheese sauce (about 2½ cups), melt the butter in a saucepan over low heat and stir in the flour with a wire whisk or wooden spoon until the flour is a light golden color. Then pour in the milk. Stir until well blended and free from lumps, keeping the mixture moving until thick and nearly boiling. Remove the sauce from the heat and add the cheese and a dash of spice. *Serves* 2 or 3

Chinese Tea Eggs

This recipe may sound quite strange and exotic to us, but it is easily made and thoroughly delicious. Here is a classic and very common Chinese dish that is eaten for breakfast, snacks, or on picnics. Try them just once, and this subtly flavored and beautifully textured "hardboiled egg" will likely become a favorite of yours, too.

6 *eggs*
1¼ *tsp. salt*
½ *tsp. black tea leaves*
⅓ *tangerine peel, or ⅓ of an*
    orange peel and
    ⅓ of a lemon peel

Boil the eggs in plain water for an hour. Cool the eggs in cold water and crack the egg shells evenly all over, leaving the shells on the eggs. This will allow the tea sauce to penetrate the surface and create interesting patterns on the eggs without over-flavoring them. Place the eggs in enough water to cover them and add the salt, tea, and fruit rinds. Simmer the eggs two hours longer. Keep the eggs in their sauce until served, hot or cold. You may find it economical to double or triple the recipe in order to provide for the days ahead since the eggs take so long to cook. *Serves* 3 to 6

Italian Fried Cheese Sandwiches

These are really cheese sandwiches dipped in egg batter and fried. These rich sandwiches, almost omelettes, are bound to become great favorites. With a well-made sauce they are splendid.

For each sandwich
French, Italian, or egg bread
Swiss or Mozzarella cheese
about 1 to 2 eggs for each
*   sandwich, depending on its*
*   size*
1 tsp. flour for each egg
1 Tbsp. milk for each egg
salt and pepper to taste
oil for frying (part olive oil)

Sauce
mild tomato sauce
fresh garlic
fresh basil
minced bell peppers (optional)
ground cloves
your choice or combination of
*   capers, sliced green olives, or*
*   anchovies*
red wine
salt and cayenne to taste

Make the sauce, about ¼ cup for each sandwich should do. Make sandwiches with just the bread and a ¼-inch-thick slice of cheese.

Beat the eggs with the flour, milk, salt and pepper. Pour the batter into a bowl a little larger than the sandwich and soak for a few minutes or until the bottom is permeated with the batter, but not too soggy. Soak the other side. Fry the sandwich in about a half inch of oil until golden brown. Turn and fry the other side. Try to seal the cheese in the bread with the egg batter, or you will have to serve the fried cheese separately.

Since these sandwiches are rich but quite mild, a very pungent and slightly salty sauce is good. Hence, the capers, olives, or anchovies. The sauce should be more of a condiment than a blanket. Pour just enough over the center of each sandwich to garnish. Let your friends help themselves to more. Buon Gusto!

Sicilian Pizza

This pizza is very thick—more of a fancy bread than a pie. It is a good treat to remember when you are cooking for a lot of people because it takes less oven space than the conventional pizza.

Dough
½ to 1 *recipe pizza dough,*
   (*page 151*) *depending on how*
   thick you would like the pie
¼ *cup Parmesan cheese*
1 *cup minced onion*
1 *Tbsp. olive oil*

Sauce
3 *cloves garlic, minced*
2 *Tbsp. olive oil*
3 *cups tomato sauce*
½ *tsp. powdered cloves*
1 *tsp. crushed oregano*
1 *Tbsp. minced fresh basil or* 1½
   tsp. dry basil
3 *or 4 anchovies, minced*
salt and pepper to taste

Topping
1½ *lbs. of your choice of cheeses*
thinly sliced mushrooms, olives,
   or other vegetables for
   garnishing

Preheat oven to 375°. Make the recipe for pizza dough but add the Parmesan cheese to the original batter along with the minced onions which have been sautéed in olive oil until golden. Drain the onions well before incorporating them into the dough.

As the dough rises, prepare the tomato sauce. Sauté the minced garlic in the olive oil until transparent and combine with the other ingredients in a saucepan. Simmer the sauce over a very low heat for about 15 minutes and correct the seasoning. Cool.

Roll out the dough to fit an oiled cookie sheet or 13″ × 9″ bread pan or rectangular flat casserole dish. The dough should be at least ½ inch thick. Flute the edges to provide a rim around the sides of the dough.

Spread half the warm (not hot) tomato sauce on the dough and sprinkle half the cheese on top. Cover with the remainder of the sauce and top with the remainder of the cheese. Garnish with your choice of vegetables and bake about 45 minutes in the oven until the top is bubbling and the center of the bread is firm.

Greek Onion Pie

This is probably our favorite pie. It has a clear, light, and rich quality that is both satisfying and stimulating.

Crust
1½ *cups sifted flour*
¾ *tsp. salt*
¾ *cup butter or margarine*
¾ *tsp. honey*
3 *Tbsp. cold milk*

Filling
3 *cups thinly sliced green onions*
    including about ⅓ of the green
    top
¼ *cup butter*
1 *tsp. salt*
⅛ *tsp. black pepper*
dash of cayenne
½ *Tbsp. caraway seed or 1 Tbsp.*
    fresh dill
1 *cup yogurt or milk*
1 *cup sour cream*
2 *eggs*
2 *Tbsp. dry white wine* (optional)

Preheat oven to 425°. Sift the flour and salt and work in the butter until the size of split peas. Mix the honey with the milk and sprinkle over the flour. Toss lightly, roll out and line the pie pan. If the dough is moist, you may press it into the pan quite easily. Flute the edges of the crust and hook the bottom part of the flutes over the edge of the pan rim so the crust keeps its shape as it bakes. Bake in a 425° oven for ten minutes.

Sauté the onions in the butter until transparent and add the spices. Blend the milk or yogurt, sour cream, eggs, and wine. Combine this mixture with the spiced onions. Fill the shell and bake at 425° for 5 minutes. Turn the oven down to 350° and bake about 20 minutes longer or until just set. Serve hot or cold. *Serves* 6 to 8 (one 9" pie)

German Onion and Sour Cream Pie

A very good response to the French quiche.

Dough
*Prepare your choice of pie crust
or prepare ½ recipe pizza dough
(see page 151) substituting melted
better for the olive oil and omit the
Parmesan cheese. Add ½ tsp.
caraway seeds.*

Filling
6 *very large onions*
1 *tart apple or quince (optional)*
3 *Tbsp. butter*
salt and pepper
*nutmeg and caraway seeds to
        taste (optional)*

Topping
1½ *cups sour cream*
3 *eggs*
½ *tsp. fresh ground black pepper*
½ *tsp. fresh ground nutmeg*
2 *Tbsp. cognac or beer (optional)*

Preheat oven to 375°. Having prepared the dough, slice the onions and the apple into very thin rings or pieces. Sauté them in the butter over medium-low heat until they are golden, turning occasionally for about 35 or more minutes. Drain the onions and apple *very* thoroughly or the pie may be soggy. It helps to pat them dry, especially if you have chosen to use a yeasted crust. Lightly salt and pepper and spice the filling to taste. Combine the ingredients for the topping.

Roll out the dough and line the pan, tucking the edges of the dough under the rim and then flute the crust as you would normally. Pat the onion-apple filling on the dough and spread on the sour cream topping.

Bake in the oven until the crust is golden brown and firm, about 35 minutes. Serve hot or cold. *Yields* one 9″ pie

Italian Cheese and Mushroom Pie

This looks more like a long flat loaf of bread than a pie. A pizza dough crust surrounds the rich filling. Portions are cut like sandwiches. A good choice with salad and soup.

1 *recipe pizza dough (see page 151) or French bread dough*
3 *onions, thinly sliced*
½ *lb. mushrooms, sliced or chopped*
3 *green bell peppers, sliced or chopped*
dash of salt and pepper
½ *cup black olives and/or artichoke hearts, sliced*
½ *lb. cream cheese*
2 *cups ricotta or small curd cottage cheese*
2 *large eggs*
½ *lb. mozzarella or Jack cheese, grated*
¼ *cup grated Parmesan*
1 *tsp. crushed oregano*
½ *tsp. salt*
¼ *tsp. freshly grated black pepper*

Preheat oven to 375°. Prepare the dough, and as it rises, assemble the filling: sauté the sliced onions and mushrooms until the onions are beginning to turn yellow, about 10 minutes. Add the green pepper, toss, and cook 2 minutes more. Drain the vegetables well. The vegetable liquid may be added to the cheese if you wish. Salt and pepper the vegetables quite lightly and stir in the sliced olives and/or sliced artichoke hearts. Combine the cheeses, eggs, and seasonings.

When the pizza dough has doubled its original size, punch it down and turn it onto a lightly floured board. Divide it in half. (We are making one large pie here, but if you wish, you can make 2 or even 3 smaller ones. Just roll out a top and bottom crust for each pie.) The size and shape of this pie may be determined by the size of your cookie sheet. Or you may use a large, long casserole dish.

Roll out each half of the dough to approximately 14 inches long and 6–8 inches wide. Place one rectangle of the dough on an oiled cookie sheet. Spread on the cheese filling, keeping it ¾ inch from each edge. Arrange the vegetables on top. A little water brushed on the exposed edges of the dough will assist binding the top and bottom crust together.

Place the second rectangle of dough over the filling and seal the edges of the pie, fluting them together. For a softer, fragrant crust, brush the top with olive oil. For a crispy crust, brush the top with cold water or egg whites. Make 3 or 4 diagonal cuts across the top of the dough.

Bake the pie immediately in the oven for about 45 minutes. To produce a crispy French bread-like crust, put a pan of hot water in the bottom of the oven and brush the pie again with water after it has been in the oven 30 minutes. *Serves* 6 to 8

Pate a Choux Foundation

This batter is a foundation for desserts, cheese, meat or vegetable pastries, and can be used for fritters, too. It's easy to make and should be included in every cook's repertoire. It gives you a light airy pastry without either baking powder or yeast. All the ingredients are quickly assembled right in the sauce pan, and the batter is partially cooked before a final baking.

1 *cup water*
¼ *tsp. salt*
¼ *tsp. sugar*
½ *cup butter*
1 *cup unbleached flour, (half may*
    be whole wheat flour)
4 *large eggs*

Heat the water, salt, sugar and butter until the mixture comes to a boil and then add the flour all at once. With a wooden spoon stir the batter briskly and turn the flame to low. Continue to beat until the batter leaves the sides of the pan, then beat a minute longer. Remove from the stove, cool a few minutes, and add one egg. Beat about 2 or 3 minutes until the egg is absorbed and the batter is no longer slippery. Add the other eggs one at a time and beat well after each addition. The pâte is ready to fill or bake at this point.

This pâté dough may be made into puffs or pies, as you choose.

Cheese Pie with Mushroom Filling

pâté a choux (*page 87*)

Filling
2 *cups sliced fresh mushrooms*
2 *Tbsp. minced green onion*
¼ *tsp. thyme*
salt and black pepper to taste
⅓ *cup grated Swiss cheese*
    (*optional*)
¼ *cup cheddar cheese diced in*
    small cubes for the top
    (*optional*)

Prepare the pâté a choux for cheese puff pie (below, page 89) with a little less cheese (or use Parmesan or Romano) and 2 Tablespoons wine.

Preheat oven to 400°. Sauté the mushrooms with the onion, then drain them very well and add the seasonings. You may mix them with the grated Swiss cheese, if you like. Spread half the pâté batter in an ungreased pie tin and spoon the filling in the center, keeping it a good inch from the edges. Carefully spread and pat the remaining pâté completely over the top to the sides of the pan. You can either swirl the top or smooth it out with a bit of water if you want a shinier crust. Bake for 20 minutes. Garnish the top with diced cheese if you wish, then turn the oven to 325° and bake 20 to 30 minutes longer or until completely set. When these pies contain the cheese filling, they may take a little longer to cook. Serve hot, right from the oven. *Serves* 6 to 8

Cheese Pie Stuffed with Shrimp

pâté a choux (page 87)

Filling
1 *cup sliced raw prawns or small shrimp*
3 *Tbsp. dry white wine*
1 *Tbsp. tarragon*
1 *Tbsp. capers*
2 *Tbsp. finely chopped chives or green onions*
dash of cayenne or Tabasco

Prepare the pâté a choux for the cheese puff pie below, but use only 2 tablespoons cheese.

Marinate the shrimp for 30 minutes in the wine, tarragon, capers, chives or onions, and cayenne or Tabasco. Preheat oven to 400°.

Drain the marinated ingredients well and combine them with ⅓ cup grated Swiss or Fontina cheese.

Spread half the batter in an ungreased pie tin or small casserole. Spoon the filling on top, keeping it an inch from the sides. Spoon and pat the remaining batter over the top to the sides of the dish and bake for 20 minutes. Garnish the top with a little cubed cheese, turn the oven to 350° and bake 20 to 30 minutes longer. Serve hot. *Serves 6*

Cheese Puff Pie

An easily made and delicious pastry that is so rich it can be considered an entrée.

⅓ to 1 *cup diced or grated cheese*
1 *Tbsp. of sherry (optional)*
dash of cayenne
1 *recipe pâté a choux (page 87)*
¼ *cup diced cheese for the top.*

Preheat the oven to 375°. Mix the cheese, sherry, and cayenne with the pâté a choux batter and spread it in an ungreased pie tin. Bake for 20 minutes, sprinkle ¼ cup diced cheese on top, turn the oven to 325° and bake 15 minutes more. Serve immediately with butter. *Serves 6*

Beans

Cooking with dry beans is a necessity for people who are dependent on a grain diet. If you will eat twice as much grain as beans (in dry weight) you can assure yourself of a proper ratio of amino acids to produce the protein your body requires. Most vegetables supply very little protein. The fewer sources of animal or dairy products there are, the more important it is to see that there is a proper ratio of beans and grains at every meal.

Beans can appear at breakfast in soy milk and tofu dishes. Coarsely-ground cooked garbanzos are good in granola. Soy or garbanzo flour will balance hot cereals. Specially seasoned beans are welcome in stir-fried vegetables. Cooked and marinated beans are good in salads. You may layer sweet bean pastas in dessert and breakfast breads.

Lime and Tomato Dal

If you like curries at all, learn to make a dal that you enjoy. Dal is much more than an Indian equivalent to refried beans; because the pea bean is subtle, it complements anything and graciously accepts any influence you care to impart. Dal can tastefully balance the grains of a vegetarian diet. It is a dish with as many flavorful perspectives as you can invent.

1 *cup urhad dal, toor dal, lentils,*
    or mung beans
3½ *cups water*
2 *Tbsp. butter, ghee, or oil*
1 *tsp. salt*
½ *tsp. cumin*
1 *tsp. ground mustard*
½ *tsp. turmeric*
½ *tsp. ground ginger or* 1 *Tbsp.*
    fresh minced ginger
¼ *tsp. ground foenugreek*
cayenne to taste
3 *ripe tomatoes, diced*
⅔ *cup diced apple*
juice of 3 *limes*
fresh basil and/or cilantro to
    garnish

Wash the dal (presoaked or not, as you choose) and simmer in water until *just tender*, about two hours or longer. Cook the dry spices and ginger in the oil for a few minutes and add them to the dal. Add cayenne to taste. Add the diced apple, lime juice and, about 6 minutes before serving, add the diced tomato. The tomatoes should be hot, but only partially cooked. Garnish with lots of fresh basil or some cilantro. This dish is also good with diced jalapenos peppers.

Just before serving you may also sauté 1 clove minced garlic in 2 Tablespoons butter and add 4 Tablespoons dried coconut and ¼ teaspoon tumeric. Sprinkle it over the top. *Serves* 4

Homous

Good as a dip for vegetables as well as the traditional spread for pita bread. A good stuffing for celery.

2 *cups well-cooked garbanzo*
    beans
½ *cup olive oil*
1 *large clove minced garlic*
¼ *cup minced onion*
3 *Tbsp. minced parsley*
3 *Tbsp. minced bell pepper*
3 *Tbsp. lemon juice*
½ *tsp. ground coriander*
½ *cup or more, ground, toasted*
    sesame seeds or tahini
cayenne to taste
1 *tsp. salt*

Combine the ingredients and put through a *Champion juicer*. Correct the seasonings and chill. How spicy this is seems to depend on the strength of the garlic and onions. Add a little more cooked garbanzos if it is too sharp for your taste. Homous is usually best the second day. *Yields* 2½ cups

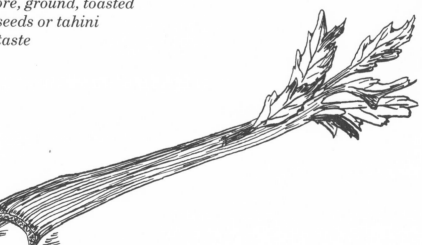

Falafel

2 *cups dried garbanzos, soaked,*
   cooked, and drained
½ *cup bulgar wheat*
2 *cups coarsely crumbled bread*
¼ *cup lemon juice*
¼ *cup olive oil*
1 *Tbsp. minced garlic*
1 *Tbsp. minced fresh cilantro or*
   2 *Tbsp. minced fresh basil*
½ *tsp. minced rosemary or* 1 *tsp.*
   ground cumin
1¼ *tsp. salt*
cayenne or crushed red peppers
   to taste

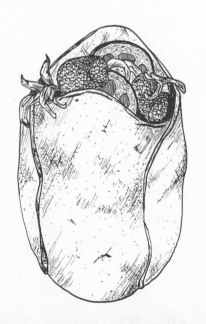

Soak the garbanzos the day before. Cook them until tender, about 2 hours. Drain them and reserve the liquid. Grind the beans fine. To prepare the falafel the next day, soak the bulgur wheat in some of the cold garbanzo liquid for 25 minutes or until tender. Soak the bread crumbs in more garbanzo water in another bowl for a few minutes, and thoroughly squeeze them dry. Drain the bulgur well.

If you have a blender, purée the garbanzos, lemon juice, oil and spices. Combine this with the drained bulgur and bread. Moisten your hands occasionally as you form the falafel into one-inch balls or small patties. Let them dry for an hour. If the falafel is too moist to be easily formed, add a little whole-wheat flour.

Fill a large heavy skillet with a few inches of oil and deep fry the balls, about a dozen at once, for a few minutes until golden brown. Serve hot. Good with a cucumber and yogurt salad, or a sprout salad. Serve with pita bread and let people put them in sandwiches with finely chopped greens.

Variation: Add ground toasted sesame seeds or try a nut butter instead of the oil. Falafel is also good served as small patties with a rich brown whole-wheat gravy.

Falafel can be made entirely with garbanzos, without adding bread crumbs and bulgur wheat, but this version has better nutritional balance and texture.

Soy Bean Patties

⅔ *cup soy beans*
3 *cups water*
1⅓ *cups rolled oats*
1 *minced onion*
2 *Tbsp. soy sauce*
1 *tsp. oregano*
1 *tsp. basil*
1 *tsp. minced garlic*
½ *tsp. salt*
1 *egg*
whole-wheat flour
oil for frying

Wash and soak ⅔ cup soy beans in 3 cups water overnight. Boil about 2 to 3½ hours or until tender. Purée the soy beans with 1¼ cups of the cooking liquid until fine. Add the puréed soy beans to the rolled oats. Let them stand for 10 minutes. Add the minced onion, spices, and egg. Mix well. Form into patties or balls and dust them with wholewheat flour. Heat the oil in a frying pan and cook them *covered* for 10 minutes on each side over medium heat. Serve with tomato sauce and pasta. Or try them with stir-fried vegetables and tamari. *Serves* 4

Refried Beans

It is always important to cook dry beans well. Refried beans, especially, must be cooked until very tender. They are a favorite of most of us. Here are three variations:

Simple Refried Beans

dry pintos, kidneys, red beans or
    a combination
water
butter or oil
salt
grated cheese (optional)

Rinse and soak the beans overnight in 3 times their volume of water. Simmer 3 hours, until done. Mash very well with plenty of butter or oil and salt to taste. Try garnishing with grated cheese.

Arizona Family Refried Beans

dry beans
milk
butter
cumin
cayenne
minced onions
garlic
Jack cheese

Cook the beans as for simple refried beans on preceding page. Drain the liquid, which you can save for soup. Mash or blend the beans with milk and butter and season with ground cumin, cayenne, and a small amount of sautéed minced onions and garlic. Top with grated Jack cheese.

Burrito Casserole

1 dozen corn tortillas
½ cup oil
5 cups refried beans "Arizona family"
½ cup jalapenos peppers, chopped
1 to 2 lb. grated Monterey Jack cheese

Preheat oven to 325°. Cut the tortillas into quarters or strips and fry for a minute in the oil over medium-high flame in a large skillet. Do not let them become hard. Drain on absorbent paper. Oil a 1½-quart casserole dish and place a layer of tortillas in the bottom, following with beans, peppers and cheese. Repeat, finishing with cheese. There should be 3 layers. Bake the casserole at 325° for 35 minutes or until hot all the way through.

Tamari Refried Beans

dry beans
tamari
garlic oil or butter
cayenne

Cook the beans and retain the liquid for soup. Blend with tamari and lots of fresh garlic oil or butter, and a dash of cayenne.

Black-Eyed Peas Louisiana Style

These black-eyed peas make a particularly savory accompaniment to corn bread or rice.

2 *cups black-eyed peas*
6 *cups water*
6–8 *cloves large garlic*
2 *Tbsp. butter or oil*
6 *to* 8 *drops or more Tabasco*
real hickory smoked salt
dash of tamari

Wash the beans and soak them in the water overnight. Two hours before you intend to serve, bring them to a boil and simmer until tender but still whole. Drain off half of the liquid. Peel the garlic, chop it very coarsely, and sauté it in the butter until nearly transparent. Add the garlic, Tabasco, and seasonings to the beans and simmer 10 or 15 minutes, stirring occasionally. You might like to garnish this dish with finely diced tomatoes (some may be stirred in) and finely sliced green onion. *Serves* 4 or more

Hopping-John

Mix hot southern style black-eyed peas (as above) with an equal volume of cooked rice. Garnish with thinly sliced green onions, and chopped fresh tomato.

Grains and Pastas

Grasses were one of the last members of the vegetable kingdom to evolve. They are everywhere today. Think of the earth and pictures of rolling fields of grain come to mind. One can even imagine the grasses as the visible nerves and senses of the earth. Appreciate grains as the *seeds* of the earth's own awareness and you can see why grains are the staff of life. Grains fill hungry bellies with the potency for real consciousness.

A well-cooked grain brings with it a primary and very pure satisfaction. Try whole or cracked grains in the place of rice for a change. Bulgur wheat is a natural companion to vegetable curries. Lightly toast barley or cracked rye in oil and boil it in stock like a pilaf. Wheat berries can be boiled until tender, washed, cooled and prepared like spanish or oriental fried rice.

Whole wheat pastas are very good with a simple herb or cheese sauce. Chow mein can be good at breakfast. A challenging dish in this section is the Vietnamese triple-noodles with vegetables. This is a good dish open to endless variations. Try making your own noodles, especially if you have never had homemade noodles before. They are great with just a little butter, salt, and pepper.

Boiled Rice

It's surprising that something so very basic as rice is rarely cooked well, even in otherwise fine Oriental restaurants. Most cooks don't seem to think it is worth their attention. Many people spend hours over the sauce and leave the rice to chance. That's not cooking.

Part of the problem is that a cooking formula that works on one supply of rice may not work on another because the age, variety, and moisture content of rice differs, even if you have bought "long-grain whole". So if you want perfect rice just spend a little time finding out how it is cooking. That's really all there is to it. Here's a method that almost always works.

Rice for Three

1 *cup long-grain white rice*
1⅔ *cup water*
¾ *tsp. salt*
1 *tsp. butter or oil* (*optional*)

Bring the rice to a boil and simmer it for about 8 minutes or until practically all of the surface water is gone and you can see bubbles on the surface. For future reference, taste the rice at this point and note its texture. Cover the rice tightly, turn down the flame to *very* low or turn it completely off. Let the rice steam for another 10 minutes or until it has absorbed all the water and is the proper texture. Toss it before serving.

The next time you cook rice, taste it at the point where the water is mostly gone from the surface and you are ready to turn off the flame. See whether it is more or less done than the last time. If it turned out perfectly last time but now seems to be softer than it was then, pour off a little water; if it is a little harder, you may add a little more boiling water. Cover and let it steam until done.

Boiled Brown Rice

1 *cup brown rice*
2 *cups water*
¼ *tsp. salt*

Rinse the rice in cold water very thoroughly. Bring the rice, water, and salt to a boil and let bubble for 10 minutes. Stir the rice once to unstick it from the bottom of the pan. Cover the rice and turn the heat to the very lowest, but not off. Let the rice almost simmer for 45 minutes longer. Toss the rice well before serving. *Serves* 3

Japanese Boiled Pearl Rice

Rinse the pearl rice 3 times in cold water. Then let it soak in cold water for 30 minutes. Drain and rinse again.

⅞ *cup water*
1 *cup washed and soaked rice*
¼ *tsp. salt*

Bring the water to a boil and carefully stir in the rice. Cover and cook over high heat until the rice begins to boil over. Turn the heat to medium and cook 6 minutes longer. Then turn the heat off, and without removing the lid, let it stand 20 minutes longer. Toss it a little before serving. This rice is very easy to eat with chop sticks. *Serves* 3

Pilaf Mediterranean

A key recipe for rice, bulgar wheat, barley, or buckwheat groats.

3 *Tbsp. oil*
3 *cups long grain rice, bulgur
    wheat, or barley*
3 *onions, chopped fine*
5⅓ *cups vegetable stock, meat
    stock, or water salted as for a
    soup*
½ *tsp. thyme*
1 *tsp. powdered cumin*
¼ *tsp. turmeric*
½ *cup currants or chopped
    raisins*
2 *cups romaine, fresh spinach,
    chard, or kale, very thinly
    sliced*
1 *cup or more condiment*

Heat the stock in a large pan with a lid. In a large skillet sauté the grain in the oil with the onions over medium-low heat until the grain is golden. You will need to keep the grain moving rapidly toward the end so it does not burn, so stir carefully and quickly. Pour the grain and onions into the stock and add any seasonings. Bring the grain and stock to a boil, turn down and simmer slowly for 10 minutes. Add the currants or raisins. Cover and simmer for 10 minutes more or until light and nearly dry.

You may also use this method to make a buckwheat pilaf if you will also stir 3 beaten eggs into the buckwheat before adding it to the oil in the skillet. Turn the grain constantly until the egg has been absorbed and cooked into the grain and proceed as above.

Have the sliced romaine or spinach and the other condiments (your choice of sautéed mushrooms, minced red bell peppers, minced fresh basil, minced fresh cilantro, diced tomatoes, tender peas, minced olives, minced clams, anchovies, or hard-boiled eggs; you may also add cooked and chopped garbanzos, or other beans, that have been sautéed in a little garlic and oil.) ready to toss with the pilaf just before serving. *Serves 8*

Dinner Rice Balls

These are good freshly made and warmed in the oven, to be eaten with stir-fried vegetables or with a soup. You can also make them small, like Swedish meat balls, and serve them with a clear chicken, cream, or soy and onion sauce.

4 *cups cooked pearl or soft*
    brown rice
2 *Tbsp. oil*
2 *tsp. minced garlic*
2 *tsp. minced ginger*
⅓ *cup minced Jerusalem*
    artichokes, bamboo shoots, or
    water chestnuts
¼ *cup minced mushrooms*
⅓ *cup nutritional yeast*
tamari to taste
dash of cayenne
¼ *cup roasted sesame seeds or*
    dried nori, a Japanese sea
    vegetable

Pour the oil into a small skillet or wok and sauté the garlic, ginger and vegetables for about 3 minutes. Mash the rice with a potato masher or knead it with your hands until it is compressed and a little sticky. You may add a little water if the rice seems too dry to stick together. Add the sautéed vegetables, nutritional yeast, and other seasonings to the rice and mix it all together with your hands.

Dip your hands in a bowl of lightly salted water and form the rice into balls, using your shoulder muscles more than your fingers. Roll the balls in the toasted sesame seeds, or strips of toasted nori* may be wrapped around the balls.

Take these along on picnics instead of sandwiches. Or put them in a bag lunch for a surprise. *Serves* 3 or 4

*To toast nori, pass a sheet of the seaweed a few times over an open flame until it becomes fragrant. That is all there is to it.

Other Ways to Cook Rice

In Greece white rice is washed and tossed with vegetables in a pan with olive oil. Then almost double the rice's volume in water is added. It is simmered 20 minutes, spiced, and left covered to finish steaming.

In China white rice is placed in an oven casserole with vegetables, such as peas and chopped dried mushrooms, and then baked in 1¾ times rice's volume of water in a 350° oven for 15 minutes. Turn the oven off and leave the rice to steam for approximately 20 minutes more.

In many parts of the world rice and other grains are sautéed in oil until golden and then cooked in a little less than twice their volume of water or stock. This is one of the best ways to cook rice for the individual grains are always fluffy and separate and the flavor is rich.

Spinach Lasagne Baked in Cream Sauce

Not the usual red lasagne. This is from the era before tomatoes were ever introduced to Italy.

1 *lb. spinach or whole wheat lasagne noodles*
salted water
8 *Tbsp. butter*
8 *Tbsp. flour*
5½ *cups milk*
1 *tsp. thyme*
½ *tsp. nutmeg*
¼ *tsp. black pepper*
⅛ *tsp. cayenne*
¼ *cup white wine*
salt to taste
⅔ *cup Parmesan cheese*
1 *lb. Ricotta or cottage cheese*
1 *lb. grated Mozzarella or Jack cheese*
paprika
minced parsley

Cook the lasagne noodles in 3 times their volume of salted boiling water until just *al dente* or 5 minutes. Drain quickly, rinsing under cold water, and lay the noodles out on a cloth to dry slightly. Make the cream sauce with the butter, flour and milk, and seasonings. Butter a large flat baking dish generously and layer the bottom with pasta. Spoon on cream sauce and sprinkle with Parmesan cheese. Spread Ricotta over the cream sauce and finish with the grated cheese. Depending on the size of your pan, you may have enough for 3 layers. Finish the top with cream sauce. Bake covered at 375° for 30 minutes.

Uncover and bake for 10 more minutes, garnish with a little more Parmesan, paprika, and minced parsley.

This dish is also particularly delicious when it is made with whole-wheat noodles and fresh spinach. Cook a pound of chopped spinach until tender but still bright green, and drain very thoroughly. Layer the spinach just after the noodles and cream sauce. Add a little more nutmeg to the sauce and top the casserole with cheese. *Serves* 6 to 10

Spaghetti with Green Sauce

A good way to serve spaghetti to accompany, not dominate, other food. The sauce is delicious on any pasta.

½ *lb. thin spaghetti* (*vermicelli*),
    whole-wheat or spinach
2 *qts. water*
2 *tsp. salt*

Sauce
2–3 *large cloves garlic*
¼ *lb. butter or* ½ *cup olive oil*
⅓ *cup fresh basil leaves, or more*
3 *Tbsp. fresh oregano*
⅓ *cup fresh parsley*
1 *Tbsp. tamari*
freshly grated black pepper
2 *Tbsp. dry sherry or marsala*
½ *cup toasted almonds*
    (*optional*)
⅓ *cup Parmesan cheese*
    (*optional*)
pine nuts (*optional*)

First prepare the sauce: chop the garlic and cook until transparent with butter or oil. Combine all the spices and the garlic butter or oil in the blender and purée until smooth. Place the spaghetti in the salted boiling water and cook until *al dente* (done, but offering resistance to the teeth). Drain the noodles and toss them with the sauce and the sherry. Garnish with any or all of the following: chopped toasted almonds, pine nuts, and Parmesan cheese. Serve immediately. *Serves* 3 to 5

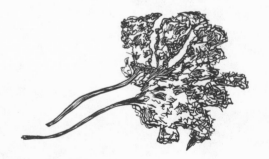

Rosemarie

This recipe is included here to introduce you to a delicious and very useful pasta called rosemarie. It looks like small almonds or large grains of rice with pointed ends. Sometimes you will find it labeled with its proper name, but you may have to look through packets of soup macaroni until you find one of them that answers to this description. Since it is a refined pasta it will not provide much protein, but when combined properly with other foods is sure to delight everyone.

Rosemarie with Peas

1½ *cups rosemarie or other small*
    soup macaroni
6 *cups salted boiling water*
6 *Tbsp. butter*
1 *cup cooked tiny green peas*
1 *tsp. minced rosemary or sweet*
    majoram, and/or thyme
2 *Tbsp. dry sherry*
fresh black pepper and a little
    freshly grated nutmeg

Boil the rosemarie in the salted water for about 15 to 20 minutes until *al dente*. Drain and toss with the butter, peas, spices, and sherry. Serve hot. See Home-made Noodles (page 108) for instructions on making your own rosemarie. *Serves 4 to 6*

Home Made Noodles

Making noodles at home is great fun, and many variations of shape and ingredients can be combined to make very special pastas.

2 cups unbleached flour
1 tsp. salt
2 eggs
1 tsp. oil and enough
    water to bring the total to ½
    cup plus 2 Tbsp.

Sift the flour and salt together into a large bowl. Beat the eggs, water, and the oil together and pour them into a well in the center of the flour. Combine the mixture well and turn the dough out onto a floured board. Knead the dough until it is smooth and elastic, adding more flour or water only if it is really necessary. Cover the dough and let it rest for 20 minutes. Roll the dough out on a floured board until it is very thin.

One method of cutting noodles is to place the rolled dough on waxed paper (or even floured newspaper) and roll it up from two opposite sides. Then slice the double roll with a knife into very thin noodles. The shape you choose for the noodles is up to you. Note that fresh noodles may stick together easily, so keep them lightly floured and loose. If you will not be cooking them immediately, place them on a floured tray, cover with foil and refrigerate. Let them come to room temperature before you boil them. *Serves 3 to 4*

See page 109 (opposite) for other variations on home made noodles.

Avocado Noodles

Quick, rich, and very avocado.

1 *lb. egg noodles, whole-wheat,*
    spinach, or soy
3 *to 4 qts. boiling water*
1 *tsp. salt*
1 *cup grated cheese, your choice*
1 *or more avocados, thinly*
    sliced
salt and black pepper to taste
1 *Tbsp. dry white wine* (*optional*)
3 *Tbsp. slivered almonds*
    (*optional*)
1 *Tbsp. minced parsley*
    (*optional*)

Boil the noodles until just tender and toss them with the grated cheese, avocado, salt, pepper, and wine. Garnish with the almonds or minced parsley and serve at once. *Serves* 4 to 8

More Noodles

Bohemian Caraway Noodles: Combine ¼ cup or more rye flour with the white flour (to make 2 cups) and add 1½ Tablespoons of chopped caraway seeds and 1 Tablespoon ground caraway.

Sesame Noodles: Add ¼ cup ground roasted sesame seeds and 3 Tablespoons whole toasted sesame seeds to the flour and prepare as above.

Herb Noodles: Add finely minced parsley, thyme, oregano, green onion or chives and a few Tablespoons of grated Parmesan cheese.

Whole Grain and Bean Flour Noodles: Prepare with any combination of ingredients and flavorings if you will also add ⅓ to ½ cup of gluten flour.

Rosemarie: Roll the dough out a little thicker than for regular noodles, cut it into very small diamond shapes and toss with flour.

Triple Noodles with Vegetables and Egg Strips

This is a Vietnamese inspired meal of many interesting flavors. It's also fun to assemble. First you prepare the noodles, the egg strips, and the sauce; stir-fry the vegetables and then assemble the dish.

1½ *ounces cellophane noodles*
  (*also known as bean thread*)
1½ *qts. salted water*
1½ *ounces udon noodles or*
  whole-wheat spaghetti
1½ *ounces regular egg noodles or*
  chinese rice noodles

Sesame Egg Strips
2 *Tbsp. toasted sesame seeds*
4 *or 5 large eggs*
1 *Tbsp. water*
2 *Tbsp. minced chives or green*
  onions
2 *tsp. tamari*
dash of cayenne
2 *Tbsp. oil*
⅛ *tsp. aromatic sesame oil*

The Coconut Sauce
½ *to* ¾ *cup unsweetened dried*
  coconut
3 *Tbsp. roasted peanuts*
1½ *cups chicken, vegetable or*
  shrimp broth

Soak the cellophane noodles in warm water until softened, about 15 minutes. Place them in 1½ quarts of boiling salted water and cook with the other noodles until done, about 4 to 6 minutes. Rinse all the noodles in cold running water and cut into manageable lengths. Set aside.

Toast the sesame seeds in a frying pan until golden, stirring or shaking constantly so they do not burn. Mix the eggs, water, onions, seasonings, and sesame seeds. Pour them into a large very well-oiled frying pan set over low heat. Cook the eggs very slowly without stirring. When they are just set, slide the eggs from the pan with a spatula and cool. Lightly sprinkle the omelette with the sesame oil. Cut the eggs into noodle-like strips about 2 inches by ½ inch and reserve.

Purée the sauce ingredients in a blender. Taste and correct the seasoning. Transfer the sauce to a large pan and keep it warm.

Put 2 tablespoons of oil in a skillet or wok that is over a medium-high heat. Add the cauliflower or broccoli, yams, onions and mushrooms, the jicama and squash and sauté

½ *tsp. honey or more to taste*
2 *Tbsp. lime juice* (*optional*)
1 *or 2 small cloves garlic*
1½ *tsp. minced fresh ginger*
1½ *Tbsp. minced cilantro*
    (*Chinese parsley*)
1 *Tbsp. tamari*
½ *to 1 small hot chili pepper,*
    seeded and finely diced
3 *Tbsp. dried shrimp or bonito*
    flakes (*optional*)

Vegetables
1 *cup cauliflower or broccoli*
    florets
½ *cup partially cooked and*
    cooled sliced yams
4 *Tbsp. minced onions*
1 *cup mushrooms, sliced*
½ *cup sliced jicama root or water*
    chestnuts
1 *cup quartered and sliced*
    summer squash
2 *cups sliced pea pods* (*snow*
    peas) *and/or green peas*
½ *lb. bean sprouts*

until nearly tender. Add the snow peas, stir a minute, then add the sprouts and stir-fry until they are just hot.

Add the sauce and noodles to the sautéed vegetables. When they are just hot enough to steam, turn them onto a warm serving dish and garnish with the egg strips and ¼ cup toasted grated coconut. Cooked shrimp makes a nice garnish, too. *Serves* 4 to 6

Home-Made Proteins

Soymilk Dishes, Tofu, Yogurt, and Cheese

It is a real challenge and a great satisfaction to make your own soymilk and tofu. And do try making soymilk. It is extremely useful and very delicious.

If you can make yogurt, then you can also make a simple cheese. If you can do these things, the possibilities for real self-sufficiency begin to open up. Good luck. We are beginners ourselves but have found our time well rewarded with a deeper appreciation for these ancient, subtle, and simple skills. Soon we will be enjoying homemade tofu or cheese nearly every day.

If you have enjoyed making your own bread, then you may find the soy-dairy a very rewarding aspect of cooking to explore.

Soymilk

Fresh, warm soymilk dipped right from the kettle, is one of nature's finest essences. It is a drink that seems to stimulate and comfort every cell in the body. Just about anywhere in the world soybeans provide the lowest cost source of high quality protein. That is true in this country also. Making soymilk is a simple process that transforms the beans into an easily digestible milk that contains more protein and less fat than cow's milk. And once you have soymilk, it can be transformed into many things, including soy cheese or tofu.

To make soymilk at home you will need a blender, mill, or Champion juicer to grind the soaked beans and a cloth and colander to separate the milk from the pulp.

Soymilk can also be made with less water, to become a base for ice cream, soups, and for anything else in which you might use milk.

The Japanese call soy pulp "*okara*". The *okara* is mostly fiber, and although it does not contain much protein, it can be used as a substitute for bran (wheat fiber) in muffins, or it can be baked with oats and other ingredients to make a granola. Okara can also be toasted and added to cookies and breads.

6 *cups water* (*not including the soaking water*)
1 *cup dry soybeans*

Wash and then soak the soybeans in triple their volume of water for 10 to 12 hours. Drain and then wash them twice, rubbing them between the palms of your hands to remove as many skins as possible. This removes cellulose and makes the milk taste less "beany."

Grind the beans with 3 cups of hot water into a bowl, or put the beans in a blender with 3 cups of hot water. (If you have a standard size blender, you may find it best to purée only ½ of the beans at a time.)

Pour the purée into a flour sack, cheesecloth, or clean dishtowel placed over a colander. Place the colander over a heavy kettle

or saucepan to catch the soymilk. Form the cloth into a sack by gathering the edges up and twisting it over the soypulp. Press the sack with a potato masher or glass jar to extract the liquid. Open the sack and scrape the pulp into a bowl. Add 2 cups of very hot water and stir it well. Pour this mixture back into the cloth in the colander over the kettle and repeat the pressing operation described above. Wring the sack out thoroughly to extract all the liquid.

Bring the liquid mixture (the Japanese call it *gô*) to a boil. When the *gô* begins to boil and foams up quickly, lower the heat and sprinkle ½ cup of cold water over the surface. Let it simmer for a few minutes and boil up the second time. Sprinkle another half cup of cold water over the surface. Continue to simmer. The third time it boils up, take the kettle off the heat.

Serve the soymilk hot or very cold with less than a pinch of salt. This is a great base for carob drinks. *Yield* 1 quart

Tofu

1 *cup soybeans*
5 *cups water*
1 *to* 1½ *tsp. nigari or*
2½ *Tbsp. freshly squeezed lemon juice*

Follow the recipe for making soymilk but use only 5 (not 6) cups of water. Prepare for making the tofu by placing a cheesecloth in a colander and setting it over a pan or bowl to catch the whey. Make a solidifying solution by adding one cup of hot water to the lemon juice or nigari. (Nigari, a mineral extraction from sea water, makes the firmest and best tasting tofu.)

Bring the strained soymilk to a boil, reduce the heat and simmer it for 5 minutes. Remove it from the heat and while stirring, pour in ⅓ of the solidifying solution. Stir it a few more times and stop. When the soymilk is still, lift out the spoon. Sprinkle the second third of the solidifier solution over the surface, cover the pan and wait 3 minutes while the curds form. Sprinkle the remaining third of the solidifier over the surface of the soymilk. *Very lightly* stir just the upper ½ inch layer of the curds for 20 seconds. Cover the pot and wait 3 minutes. The soymilk should be completely separated into curds and whey. If not all the soymilk has curdled, add a small quantity of solidifying solution and stir very gently.

Put a fine-mesh strainer into the surface of the curds and dip out a little whey to moisten the cheesecloth. Gently ladle layers of the curds into the cloth. Fold the edges of the cloth over the curds and set a one pound weight on top for 15 minutes or until the whey no longer drips from the colander. A pan of water can be used for the weight.

Fill a large container or very clean sink with cold water. Remove the weight from the tofu. Turn the colander over into the water, holding the top of the cloth sack, and carefully unwrap the tofu. Cut the tofu in half. Let the tofu

remain in the water until firm, about 5 minutes. Lift it out by slipping a plate under the tofu. If the tofu is not to be used immediately, store it in the refrigerator immersed in cold water.

Kinugoshi

This is a very delicate, almost silken, soy custard. We enjoy it with any meal, but particularly at breakfast. The soy protein combines very well with our morning breakfast cereals.

3½ cups thick soymilk
honey to taste (*optional*)
¼ teaspoon very finely minced
    lemon peel
4 tsp. lemon juice
2 Tbsp. water

Prepare soy milk (page 114) using only 5 (not 6) cups of water. Put a large serving bowl in a place where it will not be disturbed for at least 30 minutes and add the soymilk. (You may sweeten or flavor the hot soymilk at this time.) Mix 4 teaspoons of fresh lemon juice with 2 tablespoons water. Stir the soymilk, and as you continue to stir the milk quickly, pour in the peel, lemon juice, and water. Stir a few seconds longer, stop the spoon, and when the mixture is still, lift out the spoon. Let the soymilk stand until cool and solidified, about half an hour.

After the kinugoshi is cold you may carefully fold in fresh fruit or thick fruit purées. *Serves 3*

Tofu-Nut Butter

1 *cup tofu*
½ *cup ground walnuts, peanuts,*
    almonds, or sesame seeds
4 *Tbsp. oil or ½ cup nut butter*
1 *Tbsp. honey or ¼ cup chopped*
    raisins and
2 *tsp. lemon juice*

Drain the tofu by placing it on a towel in a container in the refrigerator for one or 2 hours. Assemble the ingredients and purée or mash them together. Serve chilled.

Tofu and Stir-Fried Vegetables

Tofu is usually cut into bite-sized pieces and tossed with cooked vegetables at the last minute. Here is a variation in presenting tofu that we particularly enjoy.

firm tofu
minced fresh garlic
minced fresh ginger
oil
tamari
vegetables
aromatic sesame oil

Slice the tofu into 2 pieces about ¾ inch wide, 1½ inch long, and ⅜ inch thick. Heat a skillet or griddle and sauté the garlic and ginger in enough oil to moisten the griddle. Place the tofu on the griddle with a spatula and very lightly brown it over medium heat. Sprinkle tamari over the tofu and the griddle and turn the tofu over. The tamari will evaporate and leave a delicious coating on the tofu. Lift the tofu off and keep it warm. Prepare the vegetables and garnish with the seasoned tofu and a little aromatic sesame oil.

Sprouted Soybean Puree

One day we remembered we hadn't cooked our soaking soybeans and found they had sprouted. We discovered a delicious and very digestible way to use soybeans. The end product is quite like soft tofu, but it is much easier to prepare. It has a unique fruit and nut sweetness.

soybeans
water

Cover soybeans with 3 times their volume of water and soak for 12 hours. Drain the soybeans and put them into a large glass jar, rinsing them 3 times a day or more until they have sprouts nearly ½ inch long. Put the sprouts in a pressure cooker and almost, but not quite, cover them with water. Pressure cook the soy sprouts for 30 minutes or until they are completely soft.

The purée can be used for spreads when combined with oil and seasonings. It can be added to humous or tabouleh, and is a nutritious thickener for creamy vegetable soups or sauces. Sprouted soybean purée also combines beautifully with hot breakfast cereals.

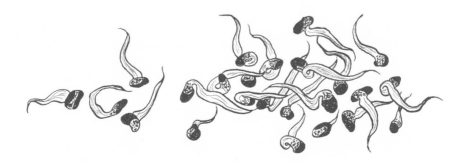

Yogurt

This recipe makes a very thick, creamy yogurt. You may want to sweeten it with a little honey or fruit purée after it has set, but we like it just the way it is.

1½ cups non-instant powdered milk
½ cup canned evaporated milk
3 Tbsp. fresh yogurt
3 cups warm water

Non-instant powdered milk is recommended because some of the available brands of instant milk inhibit proper setting.

Purée the ingredients in a blender. Let this mixture stand for 5 minutes or longer and lift off the froth. Pour the mixture in a glass jar and cover. Depending on the temperature, it will take from 4 to 5 hours to set. If you do not have a blender or an electric mixer, a wire whip may do the trick, just so long as the powdered milk is not at all lumpy. If the powdered milk has not been dissolved completely, the yogurt may have a granular texture.

An oven with a strong pilot light will often work as an incubator. Set the jar in very warm water and check the temperature inside the oven from time to time. (A good temperature to ripen yogurt is 110°F.) If the pilot is not producing enough heat you might have to turn on the oven to its lowest setting for a few minutes out of every 40. You can usually find a system that will work in every kitchen without buying an incubator, although they really do make yogurt production easy and predictable. *Yields* 5 cups yogurt

Yogurt Cheese

Place yogurt in a cheesecloth and suspend it above a dishpan for a few hours or longer. Simple, isn't it? This is a little like cream cheese and is good with minced golden raisins and other dried fruit that has been softened in juice. It can also be used for spreads and dressings.

Simple Cheese

This is a little like cottage cheese and is very easy to make.

4 *cups fresh whole milk or reconstituted whole milk made with twice the usual amount of non-instant milk powder*

2 *Tbsp. freshly squeezed lemon juice or 1 rounded tsp. nigari dissolved in ½ cup hot water*

Mix the powdered milk with the whole milk and pour it into a saucepan. Bring the milk to the scalding point (about 150°) over a low flame. Remove the milk from the heat. Stir in the lemon juice or nigari dissolved in hot water. Cover the mixture and let it stand in a warm place until the curds taste good to you, anywhere from 2 to 8 hours.

Pour the curds and whey through a double layer of cheesecloth set in a colander. Catch the whey in a bowl and use it for soups or breads. Allow the curds to drain and dry for a few hours and then refrigerate. You may add a dash of salt and some cream to the curds, cook with them, serve them with applesauce, or experiment. *Yields* 1 cup

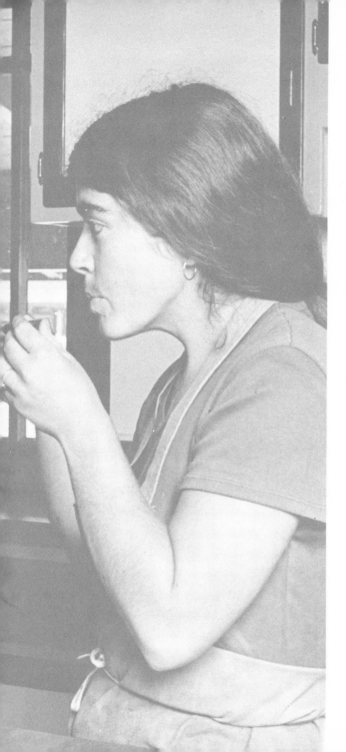

Sauces and Chutneys

In a vegetarian diet, especially when many beans and grains are eaten, a good sauce can make all the difference between just plain "rice and beans" or an intriguing Mexican, Indian or "Szechuanese" dinner. The sauce can also help balance the protein in the meal.

Remember that spices vary enormously in the strength and quality of their flavor, so all the suggested seasonings should be carefully tasted to see how they suit you. Even tamari differs considerably in the strength of its flavor and in its salt content. So when you make these sauces we would suggest that you add, perhaps, a little less than is called for and then increase the elements until the balance is right.

Apple Cider Sauce

3 cups tart apples sliced in ¼
    inch pieces
4 cups apple cider*
honey or brown sugar to taste
    (optional)
1 tsp. cinnamon
½ tsp. ground coriander, or ½
    tsp. cardamon and 1 tsp.
    nutmeg
3–3½ Tbsp. cornstarch

Slice the unpeeled apples and drop in a pan with all but one cup of the apple cider. Bring them to a simmer and when the apples are cooked thoroughly, but not yet mushy, sweeten and add the spices. Add the cornstarch which has been dissolved in the remaining apple cider. Bring to a boil and serve. The sauce should be pretty thick. Serve hot. *Yields* about 6 cups

Avocado Sauce

Good over omelettes and sliced hard-boiled eggs on toast. Delicious with rice and vegetable dishes.

2 Tbsp. minced onion
2 Tbsp. butter
1 small green chile pepper,
    seeded and diced or
¾ tsp. crushed red peppers (to
    taste)
½ cup milk
2 avocados, peeled, seeded and
    diced
salt to taste
a little nutmeg, cilantro, sesame
    oil, etc. to taste

Sauté the onion in the butter with the seeded and diced chile, about 3 minutes. Add the milk and heat slowly. Put the avocado through a wire strainer or purée in a blender. Add the avocado to the very hot milk sauce. Season. Thin the sauce with a little more milk if necessary. Serve immediately. *Yields* about 3 cups

*Note: This recipe works well for any fruit and its juices: i.e., pineapple, apricots, oranges and strawberries. Adjusting the amount of cornstarch will thicken or thin the sauce to suit its use. Try a little cardamon and dry sherry for the lighter fruits.

Szechuan-Style Black Bean Sauce

This is a rich and rewarding sauce. Excellent stirred with your choice of a single braised vegetable. This is also a welcome condiment to have on hand.

¼ *cup black beans*
2½ *cups vegetable or meat stock*
7 *tomatoes, medium sized and ripe*
1 *medium eggplant*
1 *cucumber or zucchini*
1 *green pepper*
1 *small hot chile*
1 *onion*
3 *cloves garlic*
2 *Tbsp. minced ginger*
1 *Tbsp. oil*
½ *cup red wine*
1½ *Tbsp. miso (white or "shiro" preferred)*
1 *Tbsp. tamari*
½ *tsp. honey (if dark miso is used)*
1 *Tbsp. aromatic sesame oil*
Szechuan pepper to taste

Wash and simmer the black beans in the stock until very soft and tender. Since this may take 3 hours or longer, you might want to pressure-cook the beans.

Wash and chop the vegetables. Sauté the garlic, ginger, and the onion in the oil for a few minutes. Add the other vegetables and stir-fry until they are quite tender. Add the mashed beans in their liquid. Add the seasonings from the wine to the honey. Simmer for 30 minutes longer. Add the sesame oil and the pepper. Correct the seasoning. The sauce may be puréed at this point or served as it is.

Serve some of the sauce with stir-fried asparagus, green beans, spinach, broccoli, or any other favorite vegetable and plenty of steamed rice. *Yields* 9 cups of sauce

Sesame and Nut-Butter Sauce

Rich and spicy, good on almost anything, and a protein-rich complement to vegetables and grains.

1 *clove garlic, minced*
1 *tsp. crushed red chiles, or more*
    to taste
2 *tsp. mild oil*
¼ *cup nut-butter*
¼ *cup toasted and ground*
    sesame seeds
¼ *cup sherry*
3 *Tbsp. honey*
⅓ *cup vegetable or chicken stock*
¼ *cup tomato sauce*
1 *tsp. vinegar*
1 *tsp. dry mustard*
1 *tsp. ground coriander*
2 *Tbsp. aromatic sesame oil*

Mince and garlic and sauté lightly with the crushed peppers in the oil. Blend in the nut-butter, ground sesame seeds, and then add the other ingredients. Stir over a very low flame until thoroughly hot. Add the aromatic sesame oil and serve.

The nut butter can be of any variety. If it is almond butter, use only one teaspoon of the sesame oil and add an extra Tablespoon of any other mildly flavored oil.

If you don't have have toasted sesame seeds on hand, you can use ½ cup peanut butter as long as you also increase the aromatic sesame oil to 3 Tablespoons total. *Yields* about 1⅓ cups sauce

Sesame Artichoke Dip

Toasted sesame seeds are a great compliment to steamed artichokes.

2 *parts oil*
1 *part lemon juice**
1 *part tamari***
1 *part toasted sesame seeds*
dash of cayenne

You can increase the toasted sesame flavor by puréeing a third or more of the seeds with the sauce in an electric blender. A little fresh ginger and garlic is also a good addition to the sauce.

*If you are ever short on lemon juice, blend some fine lemon peel into the sauce and add a little vinegar.
**You may want to use either more or less tamari—depending on its salt content.

Raw Chile and Tomato Sauce

8 *firm ripe medium tomatoes*
2 *large cans chopped green*
  chiles
½ *cup minced fresh onions*
1 *clove minced garlic*
1½ *tsp. salt*
chile peppers, minced and
  seeded, to taste
1 *Tbsp. chopped cilantro*
  (*optional*)
1 *Tbsp. vinegar*

Chop the tomatoes in very fine pieces and combine with the other ingredients, except the chile peppers. Make sure they are all finely diced. Add the fresh minced chile peppers, carefully tasting as you go, to reach the strength you like best.

Serve this sauce in small bowls at the table so it is easily available to each person. A good sauce for dipping pieces of fried tortillas. *Yields* 4 cups

Salsa Mole Vegetariana

This is a vegetarian version of a wonderfully rich and spicy Mexican meat sauce. Make it ahead of time to transform brown rice and steamed vegetables into a feast.

3 *Tbsp. oil*
1 *large onion, chopped*
1 *clove garlic, minced*
½ *cup tomato sauce*
4 *Tbsp. peanut butter*
3 *cups unseasoned broth*
4 *Tbsp. raisins, chopped dates,*
    or dried figs
1½ *Tbsp. ground cumin*
1 *Tbsp. paprika*
2 *tsp. oregano*
About 2 tsp. crushed red pepper
    or cayenne to taste
⅛ *tsp. ground cloves*
¼ *tsp. ground nutmeg*
⅛ *tsp. ground anise or fennel*
1½ *squares (1½ ounce)*
    unsweetened chocolate or
    1 *Tbsp. cocoa*
1 *tsp. honey*
2 *Tbsp. light tamari*
2 *Tbsp. ground or whole toasted*
    sesame seeds
4 *fried tortillas, crumbled*
1 *Tbsp. nutritional yeast*

Sauté the onions and garlic in a 1½ quart saucepan. Add the tomato sauce and peanut butter. Mix in the stock. Add all the other seasoning ingredients. Cook over a low flame about ten minutes. Cool slightly. Whirl half of this mixture at a time in a blender. Strain, if you wish, and then reheat in a saucepan. Correct the seasoning (especially the salt) and serve. *Yields* 5 cups

Salsa Verde

A classic sauce for enchilladas, meats, or rice and vegetables that is especially good when also served with sour cream.

1 *medium onion, chopped*
1 *clove garlic, minced*
2 *tsp. oil*
3½ *cups vegetable or chicken stock*
¼ *cup chopped fresh tomatillos**
   (2 10-ounce cans)
1 *Tbsp. fresh cilantro*
1 *Tbsp. fresh parsley*
2 *Tbsp. fresh basil*
1 *Tbsp. fresh oregano*
1, 2 *or more small green chiles, seeded and diced finely*
salt to taste

Sauté the onion and garlic in the oil in a 1½ quart sauce pan. Add the stock and the chopped tomatillos or golden tomatoes. Add the other seasonings and simmer about 15 minutes. Cool slightly and purée in a blender or press through a wire sieve. Adjust the seasoning. Pour the heated sauce over your entré and garnish with sour cream. *Yields 7½ cups*

*Tomatillos are a special variety of green tomato. They are about the size of a walnut and are covered with a thin husk-like sepal. If you have ever seen anything like them in a grocery it was probably the real thing. You *can* use regular green tomatoes, but it's not recommended. Try one of the yellow or golden hybrid tomatoes if there are no other alternatives.

Miso and Tahini Spread

Good on whole-wheat bread or as a dip for raw vegetables.

1 *cup tahini*
¼ *cup miso* (*shiro or*
    white miso is good)
¼ *cup finely minced onion*

Mix the miso and tahini together and stir in the minced onions. Let it mellow a few hours or overnight and serve. Protein rich and delicious. Also try dark miso and ground, roasted sesame seeds. *Yields* 1½ cups

Blender Hollandaise

3 *egg yolks*
1½ *Tablespoons lemon juice*
⅛ *tsp. salt or to taste*
pinch of cayenne
½ *cup butter*

Separate the eggs and save the whites for another recipe. Squeeze the lemon juice. Pour the yolks and lemon juice into a blender and add the salt and cayenne. Blend a few seconds. Heat the butter in a small pan until it is hot and bubbling, but not brown. Turn the blender on low and very gradually pour a thin stream of bubbling butter into the yolks. Blend until very thick. The sauce can be used immediately or very carefully reheated and beaten lightly with a wire whisk.

If you like more lemon flavor in this sauce, you may blend in a little shaved lemon peel with the yolks. Once the sauce is thick you may also stir in a little sherry. *Yields* about ¾ cup

Soymilk Dressing

½ *cup soymilk*
½ *cup mild oil*
juice of 1 *lemon*
½ *tsp. salt*
1 *or* 2 *cloves garlic, crushed and juiced*
¼ *to* ½ *tsp. fresh dillweed*

Combine the soymilk with half the oil and blend for a minute. Slowly add the rest of the oil as you blend. When it is thick, stir in the remaining ingredients.

You might like to vary the seasoning by adding: (1) basil, chopped green onions or chives, green olives, cayenne, and garlic; (2) a little shaved lemon peel, chopped sweet pickle, dry mustard, and salt; (3) curry powder, garlic, and salt; (4) 2 Tablespoons sherry, ½ teaspoon tarragon, dash of cayenne, and dash of tamari; (5) crushed garlic, minced ginger, sesame oil, and cilantro. *Yields* about 1 cup

Apple-Raisin Chutney

This chutney is easily made the day you intend to use it.

6 *cups chopped apples*
1 *cup apple juice or water*
½ *cup honey or more*
½ *cup cider vinegar*
1½ *or more cups raisins*
½ *cup minced onion*
1½ *tsp. cayenne, or crushed chiles, to taste*
1 *tsp. or more powdered cloves*
1 *tsp. allspice or coriander*

Combine the apples with the juice and simmer slowly for 20 minutes. Add the other ingredients and simmer 1 hour or longer. Correct the seasonings and serve hot or cold. *Yields* 8 cups

Sweet Bean Paste

This is widely used in the Orient on custards, desserts, or in pastries. It is usually kept on hand to season other sauces. Layer it in coffeecakes or try a spoonful in the center of a muffin batter. As strange as "bean paste" may sound to the Western ear, we have found that everyone, without exception so far, is quite fond of its taste.

1 *cup well-cooked, soft, aduki
     beans or small red beans*
⅓ *to* ⅔ *cup honey*
¼ *cup shortening or butter*
½ *tsp. ground star anise or
     fennel seed (optional)*
*You may add any of the following
     seasonings:*
1 *tsp. ground cinnamon*
½ *tsp. minced fresh ginger*
½ *tsp. lemon juice or light sherry*

Drain the beans, mash them well, and cook them over low heat while stirring until nearly dry. Add the honey and the butter or shortening and cook 5 minutes longer. Add the seasonings, if any. Allowing it to sit a day before it is used improves the flavor.

When the paste is thinned with a little apple juice or light sherry it becomes a sauce.

When the paste is mixed with half its volume of ground and toasted sesame seeds, a little aromatic sesame oil, and a little more honey, it is a delicious filling for coffeecakes, turnovers, or steamed Chinese dumplings. *Yields* about 1½ cups

Savory Coconut Sauces

These coconut-based sauces are a distinctive element in the cuisine of Southeast Asia, from Indonesia to India. They are a very refreshing alternative to our oily salad dressings and sugar-based chutneys.

Coconut Sauce Base

1 *cup dried, unsweetened coconut*
¾ *cup water*
1 *tsp. salt*
¼ *to* ½ *cup lemon or lime juice*
2 *tsp. honey*

Combine and purée in a blender until smooth.
Yields 2 cups

Vietnamese Cold Vegetable Dressing

This is good on a green salad with sliced crisp root vegetables. It is also good on a cold rice and vegetable salad.

1 *recipe coconut sauce base*
2 *tsp. minced fresh garlic*
2 *tsp. grated or minced fresh ginger*
1 *hot red or green chile, seeded and diced, try* ½ *of one, or more*
¼ *cup or less fresh cilantro*
3 *Tbsp. minced onion*
¾ *cup chicken, fish, or vegetable stock, or even apple juice*
salt to taste
¼ *cup or more fresh or dried shrimp* (optional)

Add these ingredients to the base and purée.
Yields about 3 cups

Fresh Fruit and Coconut Chutney

1 *recipe coconut sauce base*
   (*page 133*)
1 *cup chopped fresh fruit: such*
   as apples, pears, peaches,
   strawberries, mangoes,
   pineapple, cucumbers,
   tomatoes, singly or in
   combination
3 *Tbsp. minced fresh ginger*
3 *chile peppers* (*to taste*)
1 *Tbsp. turmeric* (*optional*)

1 *Tbsp. nutmeg or ground*
   coriander seeds
1 *tsp. ground cloves*
3 *Tbsp. honey*
1½ *cups additional fruit*

Add the fruit, seasonings, and honey to the coconut sauce base. Very coarsely mash these ingredients together and pour over an additional 1½ cups or more finely diced fruit. Let it stand at least 2 hours before serving. *Yields 5½ cups*

Kim Chee

An easily-made oriental spiced cabbage pickle that is fermented in glass jars in the sunshine. A delicious addition to vegetarian cooking. We have found that Kim Chee becomes a favorite dish in a very short time.

3 *lb. firm, very fresh Chinese*
   (*Nappa*) *cabbage*
3½ *Tbsp. salt*
2 *Tbsp. minced fresh garlic*
⅓ *cup finely chopped green onion*
2 *small red hot chiles, minced*

Cut the cabbage into pieces a little over an inch square. Put them in a flat pan and toss with the salt. Cover with a lid that can press the cabbage down and put on a weight to hold it firm. Let it stand for one morning or overnight until quite wilted, tossing again once halfway through the process.

    Drain off the excess liquid and combine with the minced herbs and spices. Pack into 2 one

1 *tsp. paprika*
1 *tsp. minced fresh cilantro*
 (Chinese parsley) or fresh
 ginger (optional)

quart jars or one half-gallon jar leaving 1½ inches or more unfilled at the top. Loosely cover the jars and let them stand at room temperature and receive a few hours of early morning and late afternoon sunshine.

Check the pickle the second day for saltiness, adding more salt if necessary. Slow bubbling should begin the third day. Let the bubbling continue for a few hours, seal the jars and refrigerate. They should keep for a month or longer. Kim Chee has a characteristic aroma that some people find a little strong. The taste, however, is quite delicious.

You can make this cabbage pickle many ways. Try a batch with the listed ingredients and dry mustard. Or, skip the ginger and cilantro and season with dill for a more Western approach.

Sunflower Dressing

1 *cup sunflower seeds*
1½ *cups water*
1 *tsp. honey*
2 *Tbsp. lemon juice*
1 *tsp. lemon peel*
salt or tamari to taste
cayenne to taste

This is a very thick and creamy dressing, slightly sweet and very good on fruit salad or on a green salad made with cauliflower and root vegetables.

The seasoning can also include dill, garlic, ginger, tarragon, and other herbs. It is good thinned with juice or white wine. Remember this dressing the next time you run out of salad oil.

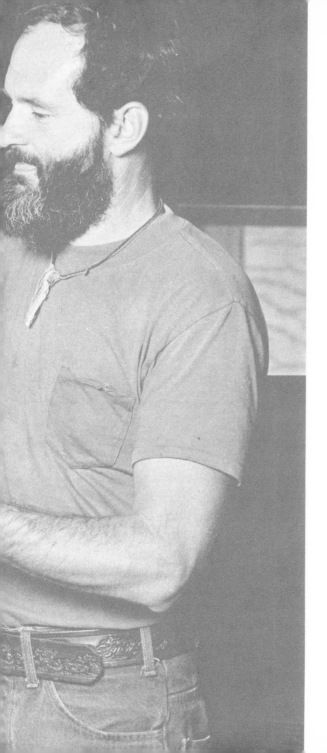

Yeasted Breads

There are few things in life that can bring such simple and wholesome satisfaction as making bread. Do grind your own flour if you can. Fresh-baked bread made from freshly ground whole wheat is so potently alive and real that it is somehow shrouded in mystery and magic.

The choice of flour is really up to you. If you enjoy a light bread, you can always substitute one-half cup of soy flour, one-fourth cup of wheat germ, and one-fourth cup of powdered milk for a cup of unbleached flour to provide more complete nutrition. If you would like to use even more soy flour, especially in a rye or whole wheat bread, add an equal amount of gluten flour to the dough and the bread will have a lighter texture, as well as more protein.

We indicate how firm the dough should be in these recipes, but since the moisture content of flours varies, be sure to use your own judgment and add more or less flour as needed.

Homemade Wheat Bread

A very wholesome and simple wheatbread, this bread is sure to have a satisfying and rich flavor if you can use freshly ground organic whole-wheat flour.

The sponge
2 *Tbsp. active dry yeast*
3 *cups warm water*
¼ *cup honey, light molasses, or malt syrup*
3 *cups whole-wheat flour* (½ *or more cups gluten flour will provide a lighter bread*)
1 *cup dry milk**
3 *Tbsp. soy flour*

To be folded in
¼ *cup melted butter or unrefined soy oil*
1 *Tbsp. salt*
2 *tsp. mace, allspice, or cardamon* (*optional*)
3 *to 5 cups whole-wheat flour*
1 *cup or more whole-wheat flour to be used for kneading*

*Dry milk increases the protein, but it also tends to make a bland loaf. Water opens up the clear taste of the wheat. You may substitute whole-wheat or gluten flour for the dry milk if you prefer.

For the sponge stir the yeast into the (very barely) warm water and allow it to dissolve for 10 minutes. Measure your choice of honey, light molasses, or malt syrup. Pour some of the yeast water into the sweetener, mix it well, and return it to the dissolved yeast. Stir the dry milk and soy flour (also the optional gluten flour if you choose) into the liquid yeast. Add the whole-wheat flour a little at a time as you stir to combine it with the liquid. Beat this thick mixture very well until it has developed an elastic quality. This will take about 100 strokes. This beating process encourages the wheat to develop gluten. A rich gluten content traps the oxygen released by the yeast, and it is these little oxygen balloons that make the bread light and high. Cover the bowl with a damp towel and set it in a warm place to rise from 30 minutes to an hour.

Pour the oil over the sponge and sprinkle on the salt. The addition of allspice or mace at this point enhances the flavor of the wheat without being noticeable in itself. These spices seem to balance the flavor of the soy flour, in particular.

Take a wooden spoon or spatula in your hand and pass it along the side of the bowl to

the bottom. Turn the spoon slightly when it is under the sponge and catch some of the dough with the edge of the spoon. Bring the spoon up along the other side of the bowl turning the dough over and folding the bottom over the top. Continue to fold the dough in this way as you sprinkle on the rest of the flour. The dough should be quite thick, eventually forming a ball which does not stick to the sides of the bowl.

Turn the dough onto a floured board and knead with floured hands. Lift the far edge of the dough toward you and place it over the other half on the board. With the heel and palms of both hands, press the dough down and away from you. Rotate the dough a quarter of a turn, fold, and knead again. Exercise your whole body as you knead. Feel your weight shift as you move back and forth over the board. Open your chest and breathe deeply. As you develop an even, relaxed, and smooth pace, the dough will become more elastic and smooth-grained. The dough should be ready to rise when it is no longer sticky and has a slightly satin sheen. It can be returned to an oiled bowl or left to rise on the breadboard, covered with a damp cloth.

Let the dough rise in a warm place until doubled in volume. Punch the dough down and place it on a lightly floured board. Divide the dough into two pieces. Take a piece of dough, fold, and knead it until it forms a rectangular piece the size of your bread pan. Pinch the seams together and place the dough seam side down in an oiled or buttered bread pan. Preheat oven to 350°. Cover the pans with a damp cloth and let the dough rise in a warm place until the dough has reached the top of the pan—about 30 minutes.

Bake the loaves in the oven for about an hour. When the bread is done it will have a deep hollow sound when it is patted with your hand. Butter the top of the hot loaves as they come from the oven. Slide the loaves from the pans onto their sides and let them cool slightly before cutting. *Yields* 2 loaves

Challah

2 *Tbsp. active dry yeast*
½ *cup warm water*
¼ *cup honey*
7¼ *to 7½ cups unbleached flour*
1 *Tbsp. salt*
1½ *cup warm milk*
    (*scalded*)
4 *large eggs, beaten*
½ *cup soft butter*
½ *to 1 tsp. ground cardamon*

Add the yeast to half a cup of warm water and let it stand 5 minutes or until dissolved. Stir in one teaspoon of the honey. Combine 4 cups of the flour with the salt in a large bowl and make a well in the center. Pour in the combined warm milk, beaten eggs and yolks, honey, yeast, soft butter, and cardamon. Stir everything together and add 3 cups more flour. Knead with oiled hands on a floured board forming a very soft and elastic dough. Don't add any more flour than necessary. The more you knead this dough, the lighter and finer the bread will become. Turn the dough into a greased bowl and let it rise until doubled.

Punch down the dough, knead it a little and let it rest for 10 minutes.

Preheat oven to 375°. If you would bake this in regular bread pans, divide the dough in 3 parts. Roll each part out into a rectangle on a floured board. Roll the dough up parallel to the longest side, fold each of the long ends underneath to meet in the middle and place in the pans, seam edge down. Let rise until doubled and bake.

Or, you may form two long braided loaves by dividing the dough into 12 equal sections. Roll each out into a long flat strip, then roll each into a tube and seal the edge. Form the loaves with the sealed edge down. For each loaf, braid 3 to form the bottom layer, 2 to form the second layer, and twist one to form the top (making a loose spiral). A little water brushed between layers will hold them together. Brush the top with a little melted butter and dust on poppy or sesame seeds. Let rise until nearly doubled and bake for 45 minutes to an hour. *Yields* 3 loaves

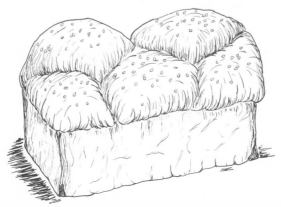

Saffron Challah

This bread was "invented" by accident. We include it here because it *is* delicious and was complimented by some people as the best they have ever eaten in their lives.

¾ *cup scalded milk*
⅛ *tsp. saffron* (*optional*)
1 *Tbsp. active dry yeast*
3 *Tbsp. honey*
4 *egg yolks*
¼ *tsp. best golden cardamon*
½ *tsp. salt*
⅓ *cup soft butter*
3½ *cups sifted unbleached flour*

Scald the milk and add the saffron while it is hot. Cool the milk to lukewarm. Add the yeast and one teaspoon of the honey. Let it sit 10 minutes and add the egg yolks, cardamon, salt, the rest of the honey, and the soft butter. Combine with one cup of the flour and beat the mixture well. Let the sponge rise a half an hour and then gradually add the rest of the flour to form a very soft dough. Preheat the oven to 175°. Knead the dough until it blisters. Form the dough into a loaf and slide it into a bread pan. Put the loaf in a warm place for 20 minutes, then in a warm oven (150° to 180°) until doubled. Turn the oven to 400° and bake 15 minutes. Turn the oven to 325° and bake about 10 to 20 minutes longer or until done. This bread, by normal standards, is "oven risen." The very warm rising provides its unique character. Serve hot with butter. This bread makes good toast. *Yields* 1 loaf

Arab Pocket Bread

2 *Tbsp. active dry yeast*
2¼ *cups water*
⅛ *tsp. sugar or honey*
¼ *cup olive oil*
2 *tsp. salt*
7½ *cups flour (if you choose*
    unbleached flour, use 6 cups
    and add ¼ cup powdered
    milk, ¼ cup wheat germ and
    ½ cup fine soy flour)
1 *cup cornmeal*

Dissolve the yeast in the water. Then add the sugar and let it bubble about 10 minutes. Add the oil and salt to the yeast mixture. Add the liquid ingredients to a bowl with 6 cups of the flour, stir, and transfer to a floured board. Knead the dough for 7 minutes, adding more of the flour until it does not stick to your hands. This dough should be a little stiff. Turn the dough into an oiled bowl and let it rise until doubled. Punch down the dough, knead it slightly and divide it into 8 pieces. Form each piece into a ball, cover them with a cloth and let them rise until doubled. Preheat oven to 450°. Roll each ball from the center out to form a circle less than ⅛ of an inch thick. You may want to cut the loaves with a teapot lid to form a perfect circle. We have found that this often assists puffing. Put each loaf on a greased cookie sheet dusted with cornmeal and let rise again until double. Put the cookie sheet on the lowest rack of the oven for 5 minutes and then transfer the sheet to a slightly higher shelf and bake for about 5 minutes more until brown and puffed. If you like, this bread may be brushed with butter or eggwhites and dusted with poppy or sesame seeds before baking. Cut open one edge of each loaf to form the pockets. *Serves* 4 to 8

Light Swedish Rye

A fine all purpose rye bread with a particularly good flavor.

2 *cups scalded milk*
2 *Tbsp. butter*
2½ *tsp. salt*
2 *Tbsp. light molasses*
1½ *Tbsp. yeast*
1½ *cups rye flour*
1½ *cups unbleached flour*
½ *cup powdered milk*
¼ *cup soy flour*
¼ *cup wheat germ*
1 *Tbsp. caraway seeds*
1 *Tbsp. anise or fennel seeds*
1 *cup or more unbleached flour*
   for kneading

Scald the milk and add the butter, salt, and molasses. When it has cooled to lukewarm, stir in the yeast and let the mixture stand 10 minutes. Sift, measure, and sift the flours once again. Mix them together and stir in the seeds.

Combine the liquid and dry ingredients. Turn the dough onto a floured board and knead 10 minutes until the dough is smooth and medium stiff. Place the dough in a buttered bowl, turn the dough over to butter the top, and let it rise in a warm place until doubled, about 2 hours. Punch the dough down and let it rise again. (If you are short on time, you may skip this second rising.) Divide the dough in half and form each half into a loaf. Place each in a buttered bread pan or upon a greased cookie sheet that has been sprinkled with cornmeal. Preheat oven to 375°. Let them rise until nearly doubled and bake for 30 to 45 minutes. *Yields* 2 loaves

Hiker's Rye

1 *Tbsp. yeast*
1½ *cups warm water*
1½ *cups whole-wheat flour (or 1*
   cup whole-wheat and ½ cup
   soy flour)
1 *tsp. salt*
¼ cup light molasses or dark
   malt syrup
½ *tsp. allspice*
1 *tsp. ground caraway seeds*
2 *tsp. soy sauce*
½ *tsp. fennel or anise seeds*
¼ *cup butter or oil*
1 *ounce unsweetened chocolate*
   or 5 Tbsp. carob powder
 2 *or more cups rye flour (slightly*
   coarse grind)

Begin by adding the yeast to ½ cup of the warm water and let it stand until dissolved. Mix the whole-wheat flour with the rest of the warm water and add the salt and seasoning. Melt the butter with the unsweetened chocolate and combine with the whole-wheat flour mixture. Add the dissolved yeast, and beat the batter well. Set it aside to rise in a warm place for about 30 minutes. Add the rye flour and knead until elastic. The dough should be a little on the firm side. Let it rise until doubled. Preheat oven to 375°. Form the dough into a loaf. Let it rise again and bake for an hour. This is good served hot with butter. If you want to take it hiking, you might try varying the recipe by adding a half cup or more of finely chopped raisins. Bring along the cream cheese. *Yields* 1 loaf

Walnut Hearthbread

Use premium dairy products and let the dough rise by the fire. A very special French bread.

7 *cups unbleached flour*
¼ *cup soy flour*
½ *cup wheat germ*
¼ *cup powdered milk*
4 *tsp. salt*
1 *tsp. honey*
⅓ *cup warm water*
1 *Tbsp. yeast*
1 *cup warm milk*
1 *cup soft sweet butter*
1½ *cups coarsely chopped*
    walnuts

Sift the flours, powdered milk, and salt into a large bowl. Dissolve the honey in the water and stir in the yeast. Allow it to activate for at least 10 minutes. During this period, warm the milk. Make a well in the center of the sifted flours and add the yeast and the milk. Blend the mixture well and then add the butter and walnuts. The dough should be stiff at this point, but if it is too dry, add lukewarm water, a tablespoon at a time, until all the flour is incorporated and the dough is smooth.

Let the dough rise at about 95° for 2 hours, covered with a damp cloth. If you haven't a warm hearth, the oven may be quite suitable.

While the dough is rising, lightly grease a large cookie sheet (or 2 smaller ones) and dust it with coarse cornmeal. When the dough has risen, punch it down and knead it for 5 minutes, saving the walnuts which fall out.

Now divide the dough into 2 pieces. Collect the walnuts left on the surface and those that have fallen out during kneading and tuck them deeply into the dough. Shape each piece of the dough into a ball and place them far enough apart on the cookie sheet so they can double in size without touching. Walnuts marooned on the outside of the dough will burn, so tuck them in the bottom of the loaf.

Let the loaves rise for 20 minutes in a warm spot, covered, or set them on the hearth.

Place a shallow pan of water on the floor of the oven and preheat the oven to 425°. When the dough has risen, bake it for 25 minutes. Remove the pan of water and turn the oven down to 300°. The bread is done when the crust is a warm golden brown—about 30 to 35 minutes longer.

This bread is best when served still slightly warm. It is delicious for dessert with soft cheese or butter and wine or tea. Walnut hearthbread easily becomes a delicious yeasted fruitcake. Try adding an additional ½ cup of honey to the dough with a little more flour. Fold in your choice of dried fruit, currants, golden raisins, candied fruit peel, sliced dried apricots, dates, or figs which have been barely softened in a little hot water and thinly sliced. *Yields* 2 loaves

Yeasted Golden Pumpkin Raisin Bread

3 *Tbsp. yeast*
½ *cup warm water*
1 *cup scalded milk*
⅓ *cup butter*
½ *cup honey*
2 *tsp. salt*
1½ *tsp. cardamon or mace*
1 *tsp. grated fresh ginger*
¼ *tsp. powdered cloves*
1 *cup cooked and mashed or*
   puréed pumpkin, winter
   squash, or yams
2 *eggs and 2 extra egg yolks or 3*
   eggs
6½ *cups sifted unbleached flour*
1½ *cups golden raisins*
   (*optional*)

Stir the yeast into the warm water and let it sit until frothy. Scald the milk and add the butter, honey, salt, spices, and pumpkin. Add the eggs and yolks to the pumpkin-milk and combine with the yeast. Prepare a sponge by adding 2 cups of flour to the pumpkin-egg mixture and beat well for 3 to 5 minutes. Let it stand in a warm place for ½ hour or longer. Add all the raisins and then the remaining flour a little at a time until you have a very soft, workable dough. Knead with oiled hands for 5 minutes. Let it rise until doubled. Preheat oven to 350°. Punch down, form into two loaves, and place into two loaf pans. Let it rise again until nearly doubled and bake for 40 minutes or until done. Brush the loaves with butter as they come from the oven. *Yields* 2 loaves

Sourdough English Muffins

These take a little advance planning and patience, but they are worth the effort. Let the starter ripen a good 24 hours or longer. Bake the muffins the next day. You can split and toast them that evening or the following morning for breakfast. These are soft inside with a real sourdough taste. Lots of little craters for butter.

Sourdough starter
1 *cup scalded milk*
2 *Tbsp. honey*

To make the starter, scald the milk and mix the honey and cornmeal. When it cools to lukewarm, add the yeast and let it dissolve.

¼ *cup cornmeal*
1 *Tbsp. yeast*
1 *cup whole-wheat flour*

The Muffin
1 *Tbsp. yeast*
1 *cup water*
1 *cup whole-wheat flour*
2 *cups unbleached flour*
4 *tsp. salt*
the starter
additional water as needed

Add the flour and beat a few minutes. Pour it into a large glass jar or bowl and cover loosely. Let it stand in a warm place, but be sure to check it in 30 minutes to see that it doesn't overflow the container you have chosen.

For the muffins, dissolve the yeast in one cup water. Then put the flour in a large bowl and mix in the salt. Spoon the starter into the flour and add the dissolved yeast. Mix the dough well. You will need to add additional water. The dough should be soft but not too difficult to work. Knead it a few minutes and then let it rise until doubled.

Punch the dough down, knead it slightly and form it into a ball. Put the ball on a board lightly dusted with flour and with a floured rolling pin roll it out to ½ inch thickness, no less. Dip a 3 or 4 inch jar into flour (or use a cookie cutter) and cut out the muffins. Set them on a cookie sheet dusted with cornmeal. Let them rise until doubled, and lift them *carefully* with a spatula onto an ungreased medium hot griddle or frying pan. Cook until the bottoms are golden brown, then turn and brown the tops. Cool, split with two forks, and toast with butter. *Yields* 12 muffins

Honey-Raisin English Muffins

You can make these in a much shorter time than their sour cousins.

2 *cups scalded milk*
2 *Tbsp. butter*
¼ *cup chopped golden raisins*
¼ *cup chopped dark raisins*
2 *Tbsp. honey*
¼ *cup cornmeal*
2 *eggs*
1½ *Tbsp. yeast*
1¼ *tsp. salt*
1½ *tsp. mace*
3 *cups unbleached flour*
2½ *cups or more whole-wheat or graham flour*
cornmeal for the cookie sheet

Scald the milk and add the butter, chopped raisins, honey, and cornmeal. When it has cooled down and is just warm, mix in the eggs and yeast. Let the yeast dissolve. Combine the salt, spices, flours, and add the yeast mixture. Knead the dough just until combined. It should be soft and just a little sticky. Turn it into a buttered bowl, cover, and let it rise until doubled.

Roll or pat out the dough on a lightly floured table to no less than ½ inch thick. Cut the muffins with a 3 or 4 inch jar or cookie cutter and lift them carefully onto a cornmeal dusted baking sheet. Be sure to keep them widely separated. Let them rise until doubled. Carefully lift them off the sheet with a spatula and onto a medium hot griddle or frying pan. (If they are stuck together, cut them apart first.) When the bottoms are golden brown, turn them over and bake the other side. Lift them off and split them with 2 forks. To toast them, spread each half with butter and put them in a 425° oven until light brown. *Yields* 18 muffins

Pizza Dough

1 *Tbsp. yeast*
1¼ *cups warm water*
¼ *cup olive oil*
¾ *tsp. salt*
½ *tsp. freshly ground black pepper (a little coarse)*
¼ *cup Parmesan cheese (optional)*
5 *cups unbleached flour (or part whole-wheat or rye)*

Dissolve the yeast in the warm water for 10 minutes. Combine with the olive oil, salt, pepper, and cheese. Sift the flour into a bowl and pour the liquid ingredients into a well in the center. Combine. Turn the dough onto a lightly floured board and knead until smooth and elastic. Form the dough into a ball and place it in a buttered bowl. Let it rise in a warm place until doubled.

American Pizza

For traditional American pizza, divide the dough in half and roll out each to fit a lightly greased pan. Cover with a spicy tomato sauce, a layer of cheese, more sauce, and grated cheese on the top. Garnish with your choice of vegetables and/or meats and bake at 425° until the crust is firm and golden and the top bubbling. This will take from 15 to 25 minutes.

For other uses of pizza dough see,
Sicilian Pizza (page 83)
German Onion and Sour Cream Pie (page 85)
Italian Cheese and Mushroom Pie (page 86)

Quick Breads

Irish soda bread, biscuits, date breads, popovers—these are all "quick" breads because they are not usually made with yeast. Quick breads should be handled as little and as lightly as possible. They resent being kneaded and many of them should be only *barely* mixed. When quick bread batters and doughs are overworked, too much gluten is formed and they become rubbery, dense, or tough.

Nearly all these breads will profit from being allowed to rest in the baking pan in a cool place for half an hour before they are cooked. The moisture has a chance to penetrate and soften the flour granules during that time and so the texture of the bread will be finer and lighter.

Use low sodium baking powders if you can. These are available in health food stores. If you do not wish to use baking powders at all, you may dissolve three tablespoons of active dry yeast in ⅔ cup or less of the liquid required in the recipe. Add the yeast liquid to the dry ingredients and let the dough rise at least half an hour in a warm place before baking.

Irish Soda Bread

We make this quick bread often, rarely measure our ingredients, and reach wildly into the spice shelf for whatever comes to hand. By the time we finish with this bread, it is hardly 'Irish' anymore. But we never have leftovers, either. It may be helpful to determine, before you begin, whether you want the bread to be light or dark, spicy or mild, sweet or salty; but if you switch plans halfway through, it will still be a winner.

3 *cups sifted flour (The more white flour, the lighter it will be. More whole-wheat or rye and it comes close to pumpernickel. Try any combination of flours that comes to mind.)*
1 *tsp. salt*
1½ *tsp. baking powder*
1 *tsp. soda*
2 *tsp. ground caraway seeds*
1½ *cups or more milk, yogurt, soup, juice, coffee, etc.*
1 *Tbsp. brown sugar, honey, or molasses (more or less)*
2–4 *tsp. cider vinegar if the liquid is not acidic*
Optional ingredients
1 *egg*
3 *Tbsp. wine, brandy, or liqueur*
½ *cup raisins or other dried fruit*
¼ *cup citron, orange peel or other candied fruits*

Preheat oven to 350°. Sift the dry ingredients together. Toss in any additions, like raisins or onions, and the spices. Mix the milk, honey, and vinegar together.

Combine the two mixtures very lightly, as if you were making a big muffin. If the dough seems a little too soft, put it in a greased or floured pie tin or skillet and garnish with seeds. If the dough holds its shape, form it into a flattened ball (don't work it too much), dust it with a nice coat of unbleached flour and put it on a greased cookie sheet that has been dusted with cornmeal. Bake from 30 to 45 minutes. Test it with a straw to be sure it's done. If you used a light hand, made it with dark flours, dusted it with unbleached flour, and put it on a cookie sheet, it will have cracked all over and you will have a splendid looking loaf.

Sometimes we make this bread with raisins, a little orange peel, nuts, caraway, and allspice—sometimes also adding thyme, sage and oregano.

¼ *cup finely chopped and sautéed*
   vegetables
¼ *cup minced chives or green*
   onions
½ *cup grated medium or hard*
   cheese
¼ *cup parsley or fresh herbs*
allspice, cardamon, sage,
   oregano, chili powder, etc. . . .
nutritional yeast
chopped nuts
seeds

Try adding ⅓ cup nutritional yeast, ½ cup chopped sunflower seeds, ¼ cup ground toasted sesame seeds and a little ground thyme or even minced onion, and a pinch of black pepper. Cut down on the sweetening and add an extra egg and maybe ¼ cup extra liquid. This makes a satisfying, rich, and meaty loaf, and excellent muffins if you add a little more liquid. *Yields* 1 loaf

Steamed Boston Brown Bread

Making steamed brown bread from scratch is not a trying experience at all, it's got to be one of the simplest breads going. And it's well worth the little effort required.

1 *cup yellow cornmeal*
1 *cup rye flour*
1 *cup graham or whole-wheat*
   flour
2 *tsp. soda*
1 *tsp. salt*
1 *cup raisins, well chopped*
2 *cups milk or buttermilk*
¾ *cup light molasses (or ⅓ cup*
   dark molasses, ⅓ cup brown
   sugar and 2 tsp. extra milk)

Mix the dry ingredients together and add the raisins. Mix the liquids together, combine all ingredients and fill greased one pound cans only ⅔'s full of batter. Cover the cans with aluminum foil and place them in a pan with one to 2 inches of water. Cover the pan with a light lid and steam for 2½ to 3 hours. Check by inserting a clean straw or toothpick into the top of the bread. If it comes out clean, the bread is done. Serve it with lots of fresh butter or cream cheese. *Yields* 1 loaf

Very Light Biscuits

These are rich, light biscuits. When made with a light sensitive touch, they are superb.

2 *cups sifted unbleached flour*
3 *tsp. baking powder*
¾ *tsp. salt*
1 *Tbsp. brown sugar*
6 *Tbsp. cold butter, or half*
    shortening and half butter
2 *egg yolks or one egg*
⅔ *cup milk, scant*
¾ *tsp. cider vinegar*

Preheat the oven to 425°. Sift the dry ingredients together and cut in the cold butter until you have uniform little pieces the size of split peas. Cutting in the butter too much will often make a heavier biscuit. Beat the egg, milk and vinegar and add to the dry ingredients, lightly tossing as you go. The dough should be quite soft but firm enough to handle. Gently mold the dough into a ball on a floured board and roll very lightly to a half-inch thickness. These biscuits are best when cut small using a 1½ inch cutter. Place them on a greased and floured sheet and chill while the oven heats to 450°. Bake them for about 15 minutes or until golden brown. Serve them right away with real butter and honey.

If you compare recipes cup for cup of flour, people tend to eat fewer biscuits than bread or muffins. But if you have made too many, these biscuits can be split, buttered and toasted the next day.

An alternative way to make these biscuits extra rich and flakey:

Roll out the dough into a rectangle and spread it with very soft butter. Fold the dough in thirds and roll it out again. Repeat this step once again. When it has been rolled out for the third time (and is ½ inch thick), cut the dough into squares or rectangles with a floured knife. Chill the biscuits for 20 minutes and then bake them in a very hot oven (475°) until golden brown. You don't need to serve these with butter. *Yields* 18 biscuits

Banana Oatmeal Muffins

½ *cup rolled oats*
½ *cup milk*
1 *cup unsifted flour, your choice*
    but part graham is very good
2½ *tsp. baking powder*
½ *tsp. baking soda*
½ *tsp. salt*
½ *tsp. cinnamon*
½ *tsp. nutmeg*
½ *cup melted butter*
¼ *cup honey*
1 *egg*
1 *cup very ripe bananas, mashed*

Preheat oven to 425°. Combine the oats and milk. Set it aside until the milk is absorbed. Mix the flour, baking powder, soda, salt, and spices together. Mix the melted butter, honey, egg, and bananas together. With a very light hand combine the softened oats, dry ingredients, and wet ingredients together. Stir until *barely* moistened. Patches of dry flour and unmixed bananas are just fine. Fill buttered muffin cups ⅔'s full. Bake for 15 minutes. *Yields* 12 to 14 muffins

Yam or Banana Bread

2 *cups flour (whole-wheat or a combination of unbleached white, graham, or wheat germ)*
1 *tsp. salt*
1 *heaping tsp. soda*
1 *tsp. cinnamon*
½ *tsp. nutmeg*
¼ *tsp. ginger*
½ *cup butter or shortening*
1 *cup brown sugar*
¼ *cup light molasses*
2 *eggs, beaten*
¼ *cup milk*
2 *cups mashed cooked yams or pumpkin*
2¼ *cups mashed ripe bananas*
¼ *tsp. vanilla*
1 *cup chopped nuts*
1⅓ *cup raisins or chopped prunes or dates (optional)*

Preheat oven to 350°. Sift the dry ingredients together. Cream the butter or shortening, brown sugar, and molasses together well. Beat the eggs and add the milk, yams or bananas, and vanilla to the creamed ingredients. Lightly combine the creamed and dry ingredients with the nuts and fruit. Turn into a greased loaf pan and bake one hour. Cooling 20 minutes enables this bread to slice easier. *Yields 1 loaf.*

Custard Corn Bread

Probably our favorite corn bread. It is quite soft in the center, almost a pudding. It has a very good flavor.

1¼ *cup cornmeal*
¼ *cup soy flour*
½ *cup wheat flour*
1 *tsp. baking powder*
1 *tsp. soda*
1 *tsp. salt*
1 *Tbsp. brown sugar or honey*
2 *eggs*
1 *cup buttermilk, or one cup milk*
    and 2 Tbsp. vinegar
2 *cups whole milk*
4 *Tbsp. melted butter or more*

Preheat oven to 350°. Sift the dry ingredients. Beat the eggs and the buttermilk together and add one cup of the whole milk. Mix the dry and wet ingredients. Coat the sides and bottom of 1½ quart casserole or large skillet with the melted butter and pour in the batter. Pour the final cup of milk in the center of the batter without stirring. Bake for about 30 minutes. The center of the bread should be soft and custardy when done. This bread is good with lots of butter. *Yields* 1 loaf

Whole Wheat Prune Bread

This is one of our fruit breads that is always received with great enthusiasm.

1½ *cups dried prunes*
1 *cup boiling water*
1½ *cups or more evaporated milk*
      or rich powdered milk
2 *eggs beaten*
1 *cup brown sugar,*
      or ⅔ cup honey,
      or ⅔ cup light molasses
½ *tsp. salt*
4 *tsp. baking powder*
3½ *cups whole-wheat flour, sifted*
      and measured; or 1 cup
      unbleached flour and 2½ cups
      graham flour
1 *tsp. your choice of spice (all-*
      spice, cinnamon, nutmeg, etc.)
½ *cup chopped nuts* (*optional*)

Preheat oven to 350°. Pit and chop the prunes. Soak them about 10 to 20 minutes in the boiling water until soft, but not mushy. Turn the prunes into a strainer and collect the prune juice. Add concentrated milk to the juice to make 2 cups liquid. Beat the eggs until they are light, add the sugar and beat until quite thick. Add the milk and prune combination. Sift the dry ingredients together and mix in the soaked prunes and nuts. Combine the dry and wet ingredients with light thorough strokes. You should have a stiff batter; however, if it is obviously too dry, add a little more milk. Turn into a large, well-buttered loaf pan and bake almost an hour. Test with a broom straw after 45 minutes. Depending on the moisture in the prunes and the batter, it can take up to 15 minutes longer to cook. Delicious hot, but easier to slice and more mellow the next day. *Yields* 1 loaf

Popovers

This is undoubtedly the all-time favorite quick bread. Make them anytime, but especially to accompany your best homemade jams. Or fill them at the last moment with vegetables in a rich cream or cheese sauce.

1¼ cups pre-sifted unbleached
    flour
¾ tsp. salt
1 Tbsp. melted butter
1¼ cup milk
3 eggs
extra butter or oil

Preheat the oven to 425°. Sift the flour, measure, and sift it once again with the salt. Add the butter and milk and beat until very smooth with a wire whisk, rotary beater or blender. Don't beat too long, however, or the popovers will be a little too dense. Beat the eggs until light and add them to the milk and flour mixture. Put a good teaspoon or more of melted butter or oil in each popover or muffin cup and coat the sides. Place the popover or muffin tin in the hot oven for about 3 to 5 minutes to heat thoroughly. Take out the tin and quickly fill each cup no more than ⅔'s full. Put the tins back in oven at 425° for 10 to 12 minutes and then turn the oven down to 325°, without opening the oven door. Check the popovers about 20 minutes later to see if they are done. These will be a little moist inside. For drier popovers, turn the oven off and let them continue to sit inside with the door open for 5 to 10 minutes longer. Popovers won't stick if your pans are well seasoned, but in case they do, run a knife around the edge of the cup and flick them out. *Yields* 14 popovers

Cheese Puffs

These are just great with soup, salad and fruit.

1 *recipe pâté a choux (page 87)*
¼ *cup Parmesan cheese*
¾ *cup diced cheddar cheese*
¼ *cup diced cheese for the top*
1 *tsp. Worcestershire sauce*
1 *tsp. finely diced chives or green
    onions*
cayenne to taste
2 *tsp. dry wine (optional)*

Preheat the oven to 380°. Prepare the pâté a choux batter and after the last egg has been added, beat in the other ingredients. Take a soup spoon and scoop up a little batter. Push it off with another spoon onto a cookie sheet. Leave enough space between the puffs for them to triple in size. Put a few cubes of cheese on top of each puff. Bake at 380° for 20 minutes, then turn the oven down to 325° and bake until firm, about 10 minutes more. Open the oven door and let them cool slowly, or serve them immediately.

These puffs may be made teaspoon size and dropped into hot deep fat. Turn them over once, drain, and serve hot. *Yields* 12 to 18 puffs

Sour Cream Coffee Cake

⅓ *cup butter*
1 *cup sugar*
2 *eggs and* 1 *egg yolk*
1 *cup sour cream*
1 *Tbsp. vanilla*
1½ *cups flour*
1 *tsp. baking soda*
½ *tsp. salt*
1 *tsp. baking powder*

Topping
½ *cup chopped walnuts*
¼ *cup sugar*
1 *tsp. cinnamon*

Preheat oven to 350°. Cream butter and sugar well, beat in the eggs and add the sour cream and vanilla. Sift the dry ingredients together and combine with the egg mixture. Grease and flour an angelfood cake pan and pour in half the batter. Sprinkle on half of the topping and add the rest of the batter. Sprinkle on the rest of the topping and bake at 350° for 40 minutes. *Yields* 1 cake

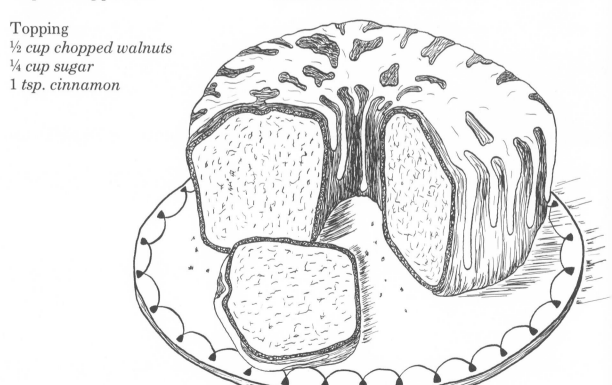

Desserts

If the meal is a little skimpy, the dessert can enrich it with more protein. If the meal is a little dull, the dessert can wake people up. If the meal is rich and heavy, the dessert can help people digest. If the meal is the last crumb in the house, the dessert can be a bouquet of flowers.

Most people start learning to cook as children by making desserts—and cooks still enjoy making them. We are leaving most of the cookies, cakes, and pies out of this book because surely there are enough recipes available by now. Please make sure your dessert complements, rather than overloads the meal. The best dessert is usually beautiful fruit, well sliced; however, we are including a few rich desserts for those occasions when you not only want the dessert to complete the dinner but also to top off the whole week.

Frozen Peach and Yogurt Cream

1 *pint* (2 *cups*) *sour cream*
1 *cup yogurt*
2 *eggs and* 2 *egg yolks*
⅓ *cup honey*
4½ *cups fresh, ripe, sweet*
    peaches, apricots, or
    nectarines
cardamon and a little vanilla

In a double boiler make a custard of the sour cream, yogurt, eggs, and honey. Stir the ingredients over hot water (not boiling) until the mixture coats a spoon. As this cools, peel and mash the peaches coarsely. Combine the peaches with the cool custard and season, if you wish, with vanilla essence and a little ground cardamon. Freeze. Let it mellow in the refrigerator for 30 minutes before serving. Garnish with more peaches.

We have also enjoyed combinations of other fruits. Try 2½ cups chopped peaches, 1 cup mashed bananas, and 1 cup mashed strawberries, or any other fruit singly, or in combination. *Yields* 8 cups

Oriental Nut Custards

These rather light, mildly sweet nut custards are new to us but we find them very refreshing after a heavy meal. Actually, here is a whole new *genre* of desserts very open to your imagination and well-suited to the use of soymilk. Please experiment.

Chinese Almond Custard

1 *cup finely ground almonds*
2 *cups water*
2½ *cups milk or soymilk*
2 *Tbsp. or less honey*
cheese cloth
2 *envelopes unflavored*
   gelatin or agar-agar

Grind enough raw almonds to make a full cup. A molineaux mill is good for this since you want to end up with almond flour. (Or, you may puree the almonds with some of the milk in a blender until *very* smooth.) Add the ground almonds to the milk and *barely* simmer for 20 minutes, stirring occasionally. Never let it boil. Strain through a double layer of cheesecloth and wring it out to extract all the flavor. Sweeten just to the point of perception if you would be traditional. Soften the gelatin or agar-agar in a little cold milk or water and add it to the almond milk. Heat until dissolved. Barely simmer the mixture for 3 minutes. Pour the custard into serving cups or dishes and chill until set.

Serve with cold, sliced, canned or fresh lichee nuts, or a sauce of orange juice and a little honey, or as is. You may also try this custard with half almonds and half dried shredded coconut or hazelnuts. This custard makes a fine condiment for meat dishes, especially lamb, when you make it with water and add 1 tablespoon chopped fresh mint with the almonds. *Serves* 4 to 6

Turkish Almond Custard

This is a sweeter and richer custard than the Chinese version.

2 *cups cream or heavy soymilk*
2 *cups milk or light soymilk*
1 *cup finely ground almonds*
½ *cup light honey or* ¾ *cup sugar*
½ *tsp. pure almond extract, or 1*
    Tbsp. rose water (If you soak
    the almonds long enough in
    milk, you don't need the
    extract).
¼ *cup rice flour*

Garnish
Choose any or all of the
    following;
1 *Tbsp. washed pomegranate*
    seeds
1 *Tbsp. finely chopped almonds*
1 *Tbsp. finely chopped pistachio*
    nuts
2 *Tbsp. finely minced soft dried*
    apricots
2 *Tbsp. finely chopped pine nuts*
2 *Tbsp. finely chopped preserved*
    ginger or preserved pineapple

Combine the cream, 1½ cups milk, ground almonds, honey, and extract. Bring to a simmer and remove from the heat. Cover and let it sit for 20 minutes over the pilot light. Strain through a double layer of cheesecloth back into the rinsed saucepan.

Mix the rice flour in the remaining ½ cup of milk and stir it into the almond milk. Simmer the mixture over low heat for ¼ of an hour stirring occasionally until the almond cream coats the spoon well. Strain through a sieve and pour into individual serving cups. Garnish with your choice of nuts and fruits, mixing just a few into the custard.

If you have a good blender you can save yourself time by puréeing the milk and almonds together until *very* fine, straining, and proceeding to follow the recipe. Try other nuts and fruits but remember that the charm of this dessert is in its simple delicacy. *Serves* 4 to 6

Applesauce Pudding

Batter
⅔ *cup finely chopped or grated tart apple or quince*
1 *Tbsp. butter*
¼ *cup bread crumbs*
2 *eggs*
½ *tsp. cinnamon*
3 *Tbsp. raisins*

Topping
¾ *cup medium bread crumbs*
½ *cup chopped almonds*
½ *cup brown sugar or ⅓ cup honey (to taste)*
2 *Tbsp. melted butter*
¼ *tsp. cardamon*
½ *tsp. freshly grated nutmeg*

Preheat oven to 325°. Chop the tart apple and sauté in the butter until just tender. Remove the apple, leaving as much butter as possible in the skillet. Sauté the bread crumbs in the skillet until a little crisp and barely golden. Beat the eggs with the applesauce and cinnamon. Combine with the bread crumbs and raisins. In another dish, mix the ingredients for the topping together.

Fill 4 buttered custard cups or a quart baking dish ½ full of the applesauce batter and sprinkle with some of the topping. Spoon the rest of the batter over the topping. Finish with another layer of topping.

Bake the custard cups 20 minutes in a 325° oven, or bake the casserole dish for 40 minutes at 350° until the topping is light golden brown and the pudding is set and almost steaming. Serve hot or cold with milk. *Serves* 4

Tahini and Fruit Pudding

Lighter than a traditional pudding—an interesting combination.

2 *sticks kanten (agar)*
5½ *cups apple juice*
⅛ *tsp. salt or to taste*
1 *tsp. almond essence, vanilla,*
    nutmeg or grated orange peel
1 *cup sesame tahini*
1 *cup or more sliced berries,*
    melon, or other fruit

Soften the kanten in the juice for 20 minutes. Simmer the kanten, the juice, and salt together until the kanten has dissolved, about 15 minutes. Add your choice of seasoning and the tahini which has been blended with ½ cup of the kanten-apple juice. Slice the fruit and fold it into the pudding. Chill.

Garnish with small pieces of fresh fruit. *Serves* 6 to 8

Old Fashioned Prune Whip

1 *lb. dried prunes*
3 *eggs*

Cover the prunes with water and simmer until tender, about 1½ hours. Cool. Seed the prunes, put them through a sieve or purée in a blender. Beat the eggs until very light, thick, and lemon colored. Stir them into the prunes. Bake in a casserole dish at 350° until light brown, about 30 minutes.

Serve with whipped cream flavored with a little lemon juice and grated lemon peel. *Serves* 6 or more

Fresh Fruit Tart Pattern

Crust

½ *cup dry unsweetened coconut
and* 1½ *cups unbleached flour.
You may substitute* ½ *cup
crushed nuts for* ½ *cup of the
flour.*

¾ *tsp. baking powder, less if nuts
are used*

⅓ *cup brown sugar*

¼ *tsp. salt*

¾ *cup cold butter*

1 *egg*

1 *Tbsp. milk or water*

Sauce

½ *cup chopped berries or fruit
(strawberries, peaches,
apricots, etc.)*

2 *Tbsp. lemon juice (if the fruit is
not tart)*

½ *cup apple juice, water, or other
juice*

⅓ *cup honey or* ½ *cup sugar*

2½ *Tbsp. cornstarch*

4 *cups berries or fruit*

To make the crust, toss the dry ingredients together and cut in the cold butter to the size of split peas. Beat the egg and milk together and toss with the butter and flour. Refrigerate the covered dough for at least ½ hour.

Preheat oven to 375°. Very lightly oil a 10 inch cake pan or German tart tin and press the dough evenly on the sides and bottom. Make small holes in the bottom of the crust with a fork and bake at 375°, 20 to 30 minutes or until golden. Cool slightly and carefully turn out to a serving plate. Place a large plate over the top of the crust, turn it upside down, and then place the serving plate on the now upright crust bottom. Turn right side up. Cool.

While the tart shell bakes you may purée the following ingredients in a blender: the fruit, juice, honey or sugar, and cornstarch. Cook this purée, stirring constantly, until thickened and boiling for one full minute. Cool slightly.

Fill the tart shell with the whole berries or medium large slices of fruit. Pour the sauce over the fruit and cool. Serve garnished with thick sweetened yogurt, sour cream or whipped cream and perfect berries or pieces of fruit. *Serves* 8 or more

Greek Yogurt Pie

One step away from cheesecake, this pie is worth pursuing. The apricot pie that follows will likely become a great favorite, too.

Crust

1⅔ *cups graham cracker, cake or*
   cookie crumbs, or finely
   crumbled stale sweet rolls
⅓ *cup ground almonds or*
   walnuts
¼ *cup brown sugar*
½ *tsp. cinnamon*
⅓ *cup melted butter*

Filling

½ *lb. natural cream cheese or*
   ricotta cheese pressed
   through a wire strainer
1 *cup plain yogurt*
4 *Tbsp. honey*
½ *tsp. finely grated lemon peel*
2 *tsp. vanilla essence*

Preheat oven to 300°. Combine the crumbs, nuts, sugar, cinnamon and melted butter and press into a 9 inch pie or spring-form pan. Bake 5 minutes. Cool.

Soften the cream cheese and blend together with the other ingredients. Spoon into the pie shell. You may serve it after refrigerating for 24 hours as it is or with a dusting of ground nuts. After the cake has set you may also top it with 1 cup sour cream, 1 teaspoon honey, and 3 tablespoons ground nuts, to be dusted on the cream or combined with it. Refrigerate the sour cream topped cake for another 10 hours before serving. *Serves* 8

Apricot and Yogurt Pie

You can transform the Greek yogurt pie into a delicious fruit pie by adding 1½ cups of sliced fresh ripe, (but not mushy), apricots or peaches to the yogurt filling. Substitute sherry or almond extract for the vanilla and skip the lemon peel if you prefer. Spread on the sour cream topping. Refrigerate the cake until set and then dust with ground almonds. You will probably make this pie more than once. This pie is also very tasty made with fresh berries.

Mango and Yogurt Pie

Recipe for Yogurt Pie
1 *envelope gelatin*
½ *cup milk*
1 *to* 1½ *cups mashed, ripe*
    mangoes
1 *Tbsp. brandy* (*optional*)
additional slices of fresh mango

Dissolve the gelatin in the milk for 10 minutes. Heat until it has boiled for 3 minutes and combine with the mashed mangoes. Add the brandy (it intensifies the mango flavor, strangely enough.) Add the yogurt and the other ingredients for the Greek Yogurt Pie filling. Refrigerate until set and finish the pie with the layer of sour cream. Chill for a few hours, and garnish with slices of mango.

Dessert Rice Balls

Rice lends itself beautifully to desserts and is extensively used for treats almost everywhere except in this country. It seems that Americans demand rich and heavy desserts and have a hard time appreciating the lightness that rice can offer. It also combines superbly with fruits and creams. The dessert rice we offer here is a modification of the traditional Japanese rice ball. Please experiment. They are a lot of fun to make.

Orange Raisin Rice Balls

3 *cups cooked day old pearl rice*
  (traditional), white rice, or
  brown rice (a little heavy)
2 *oranges*
honey to taste
½ *cup raisins and/or golden*
  chopped dates
a few whole almonds or dates
¾ *cup toasted coconut*

The rice should be tender and at least 12 hours old. Pearl rice is glutinous and forms a ball without any trouble. Brown or white rice calls for some additional honey or light molasses to stick it together. Juice the oranges and cut the peel of one into small pieces. Put the peel in the juice and cook it with an equal amount of honey for about an hour or until quite tender. Cool. Mix the peel and liquid with the rice and dried fruit and see if it is sweet enough. We enjoy this only slightly sweet. Wet your hands in a bowl of salted water and take a small handful of rice. Put a date or almond in the rice and form a ball around it, taking a little more rice if needed. Squeeze the ball firmly. Keep your hands wet and the balls will be easy to form. Roll the balls in golden toasted coconut and chill. *Serves* 4 to 6

Toasted Almond Rice Balls

Add honey or light molasses and finely chopped roasted almonds to the mix. Try finely diced dried apricots and a little crystalized ginger. Roll in more toasted almonds. Or try making these with ground or whole toasted sesame seeds. *Serves* 4 to 6

Swedish Breadcrumb Apple Cake

Good hot or cold with ice cream or a custard sauce. This apple cake is traditionally garnished with raspberry jelly and whipped cream.

1½ *cups butter*
1½ *to 2 cups small bread cubes
    and crumbs*
1 *cup brown sugar or* ⅔ *cup dark
    honey*
6 *large apples*
1 *Tbsp. water*
peel of ½ *lemon*
1 *tsp. cinnamon*
½ *tsp. cardamon*

Preheat oven to 350°. Melt the butter in a skillet and toss in the crumbs. Fry them over medium heat, stirring as you go. Add half the sugar and set aside. If you have chosen to use honey, don't add it yet. Core the apples and slice them thinly. Put them in a frying pan with the other half of the sugar and a Tablespoon of water and cook them gently with the shaved lemon peel and spices until just soft. Now add the honey. Layer the ingredients in a buttered casserole ending with the bread crumbs. Bake until heated through and set, about 15 minutes. Turn out on a serving plate. *Serves* 6 to 8

Cream Puffs

These need not be so sweet that you feel you should never make them at all. There's no sugar in the puff and the filling is up to you.

1 *recipe pâté a choux* (*page 87*)
custard, cream cheese and fruit,
    whipped cream, etc.

Preheat oven to 400°. Scoop up the batter with a teaspoon or Tablespoon (depending on the size of puff you want) and push it onto an ungreased cookie sheet. If you want the surface of the puffs to be smooth after they are baked, wet the spoon between puffs. Leave enough room between them on the sheet so they can triple in size without touching.

Place them in the oven for 10 minutes, turn the oven down to 350° and bake about 20 to 30 minutes longer or until firm. Turn off the oven, open the door, and let them sit for a few minutes before moving to a draft free corner of the kitchen to cool. Slice off the tops, remove the filaments, and stuff with custard, cream cheese and fruit, or whipped cream.

The puffs can be made any size, up to just filling a pie pan and baking it whole. Split the puff, fill, and cut into wedges. This is not bad stuffed with fresh fruit marinated with wine and mixed with cream cheese.

Try beaten Ricotta cheese, very small semi-sweet chocolate bits and chopped glacéed fruit. Try sunflower, honey and tofu spread, ice cream, sherbert, or frozen yogurt. *Yields* 12 or more

Brandied Granola Bars

6 *cups homemade granola*
1 *cup extra seeds and nuts*
   (*walnuts are particularly*
   good)
1½ *cups oil, or melted butter*
5 *large eggs*
¾ *cup honey* (*depending on the*
   sweetness of your granola)
dash of salt
3 *Tbsp. grated orange skin*
⅓ *cup brandy, or 2 tsp. vanilla*

Preheat oven to 325°. Combine the ingredients and press firmly into a buttered 9 × 13″ baking pan. Bake for 20 minutes or until set. Cut into bars while hot, and carefully lift them from the pan before they are too cool. You can sprinkle on a little more brandy if you are planning a very long hike. *Yields* 12 or more

Pate a Choux Fruit Fritters

1½ *cups chopped or sliced fruit:*
   pears, bananas, pineapple or
   apples are good
⅓ *cup honey or sugar*
1 *recipe pâté a choux*
2 *Tbsp. liqueur* (*optional*)

Marinate the fruit with the honey. Drain, reserving the liquid for a sauce. Combine the pâté with the fruit and liqueur. Drop the batter a tablespoon at a time in deep hot fat. Turn when they are golden brown on one side. Drain and serve with a fruit sauce or honey and yogurt or sour cream.

Date and Beet Cake

This cake is sweet, moist, and good just as it is without an icing or topping.

¾ *cup oil*
⅔ *cup honey*
4 *beaten eggs*
1½ *cups grated carrots or*
   zucchini
1½ *cups grated fresh beets*
1 *cup unbleached white flour*
1 *cup whole-wheat flour*
1 *tsp. baking powder*
1 *tsp. baking soda*
2 *Tbsp. cinnamon or mace*
½ *tsp. powdered cloves*
1 *tsp. salt*
¾ *cup very finely chopped dates*
½ *to* 1 *cup chopped walnuts or*
   sunflower seeds

Preheat oven to 325°. Beat the oil, honey, and eggs together until smooth. Stir in the grated vegetables. (You can make this cake with 3 cups of beets and omit other vegetables if you prefer.) Sift the dry ingredients together and gradually combine them with the vegetable mixture, dates and nuts. Bake in a buttered and floured 9 × 13 inch pan at 325° for 40 to 50 minutes. Or, for a special touch, try baking it in a buttered and floured bundt pan for an hour and 10 minutes. *Serves* 8 or more

Baklava

The richest and sweetest of all desserts.

1 *lb. filo dough*
1 *lb. unsalted butter*
1 *lb. finely chopped almonds*
1½ *lb. finely chopped walnuts, or*
    pistachio nuts (you may use
    all walnuts, 2½ lb. total)
⅔ *cup brown sugar*
1 *tsp. ground cinnamon*
1 *tsp. ground cloves*
2 *tsp. mace*
pinch of salt

Syrup:
1 *cup honey*
1 *cup water*
1 *cup sugar*
2 *cinnamon sticks*
1 *grated orange peel (just the*
    very edge of the skin)
½ *grated lemon peel (just the*
    very edge of the skin)
1 *tsp. almond extract, vanilla*
    essence, or cognac

Preheat oven to 350°. Butter a 9 × 13 × 2 inch baking pan and place a layer of the filo on the bottom. Brush the dough with the melted unsalted butter. Continue with this procedure until you have 12 layers. Mix the finely chopped nuts with the sugar, spices, and pinch of salt. Sprinkle them thinly on the last layer of buttered filo. Add another piece of filo, butter, and sprinkle on more nuts. Continue until the nut mixture is gone and you have 6 to 10 more sheets of filo left. Place the remaining filo, layer after buttered layer, over the top. Carefully cut the baklava with a sharp knife into diamond shapes, only cutting in a ¼ of an inch. Bake at 350° one hour to 1½ hours or until done.

As the baklava bakes, prepare the syrup. Combine all the ingredients except the essence in a saucepan and simmer for half an hour. When the baklava is removed from the oven, add the essence to the syrup and pour it over the top. Finish cutting it into diamonds while still very warm. Cool and serve. This is often best the second day. *Yields* 20 or more pieces

Food from the Top of the World

These are a few favorite recipes that we prepare on special occasions. Some of them actually duplicate Tibetan food; others adapt the spirit of Himalayan cuisine to our ingredients and tastes. There are rewarding skills to be learned in the folding of Moh Moh and Baos. The experimenting westerner may find as much delight as the Tibetan cook in stuffing small and delicious treasures into these pastries.

Since the climate can be exceptionally strenuous in the Himalayas, the Tibetans count themselves lucky to have meat when it is available. We present some of the traditional recipes (substituting beef for yak,) but you may find that the cheese stuffings are perhaps even more exotic and delicious.

Moh-Moh

These savory stuffed noodle dumplings are probably the national favorite of Tibet. Once you learn the simple skill of stuffing and folding, they are easily and quickly made. The meat filling is traditional, but we thoroughly enjoy them stuffed with cheese.

Meat filling
½ *lb. lamb, beef, or both*
2 *Tbsp. tamari*
2 or 3 *cloves garlic, finely minced*
½ *tsp. fresh ginger, finely minced*
    (optional)
1 *Tbsp. fresh cilantro, finely*
    minced (optional)
2 *tsp. water*
10 *drops Tabasco*
1 *cup total of any or all of:*
    minced celery, spinach or
    mushrooms

Moh-Moh noodle dough
2 *cups unbleached flour*
⅔ *cups water*

Chop the meat, including some of the fat, into fine pieces about half the size of a split pea. Put it into a bowl and add the seasonings and water. Mince the vegetables and stir them into the meat, pressing the mixture together. To prepare a cheese and vegetable filling, use the same ingredients as those listed above, *except* omit the meat and use about one cup of finely diced Swiss cheese, Icelandic milk cheese, or diced (not grated), Romano. Add a little more garlic and Tabasco and 1 teaspoon aromatic sesame oil.

Stir the water into the flour in a large bowl until it forms a ball. Knead the dough in the bowl for a minute and then transfer to a board and knead two minutes longer. Fold the dough into a log about a foot long and cut it into inch-wide pieces. Roll each piece into a ball between the palms of your hands and flatten it on a bread board that has been lightly dusted with flour. Roll the dough into a small circle about 2½ inches in diameter, then take the rolling pin and roll from the outside edge toward the center. Press down on the edge of the circle with the rolling pin to make it very

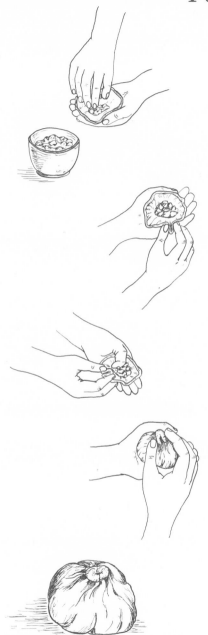

thin and roll with increasingly less pressure as you reach the middle so that the middle of the dough is thicker.

Holding a piece of rolled-out dough in one hand, place one or two heaping Tablespoons of the filling in the center. With the thumb and forefinger of the other hand, take hold of the edge of the dough and pinch the edge toward the thumb. Keep the thumb in the same place as you continue to pinch the dough together. Twist the moh-moh toward your folding hand as you continue to pleat the dough, stretching the dough over the filling.

Place the moh-moh on a well-greased steamer pan and steam for 20 minutes. Or, you may steam them for 15 minutes and keep them in the cold steamer for a few hours, steaming again for an additional 5 to 7 minutes just before serving.

If you do not have a steamer, you will need a pie plate with holes in the bottom, a few old tuna cans or small heat-proof cups or bowls, and a large pan with a lid. Grease the pie tin and place the moh-moh on the surface. Put the tuna cans or cups in the bottom of the pan and fill the pan ⅔'s to the top of the cans or cups. Place the pie tin on top of the cups, heat the water to a fast boil, and cover. Steam the moh-moh as usual.

Moh-moh served with a clear meat soup is traditionally considered to be a complete meal. *Serves* 2 to 4

Bao Dough

Buns made from this yeasted dough, filled with meat or vegetables, and steamed are delicious!

½ *cup scalded milk*
½ *Tbsp. yeast*
2 *Tbsp. honey*
1 *Tbsp. shortening or lard*
2 *cups sifted unbleached flour*

Fillings
Chinese cabbage or spinach,
   finely chopped
tofu or hard scrambled egg
sautéed mushroom
sautéed onions (*crisp*)
minced garlic
Tabasco
minced cilantro
minced ginger
oyster sauce or miso
tamari
aromatic sesame oil
   (*recommended*)

Scald the milk and let it sit until lukewarm. Stir in the honey and the yeast. While the yeast dissolves, cut the shortening finely into the flour. When the yeasted milk is bubbly, stir it into the flour. Knead this stiff dough for a few minutes and let it rise in a covered bowl until nearly doubled, about an hour. Knead the dough once again, cover, and let it rise until doubled.

The amount of filling is up to you—it depends on how much filling you like and how much stuffing your skill enables you to get into the dough. Try sweet bean paste (see page 132) as a snack or for dessert. Chopped dates, nuts, and fruit also make a good dessert filling.

For a vegetarian filling make a mixture of any or all of the ingredients and spices listed.

Or for a meat filling use moh-moh filling (see page 182) or any chopped meat or fish seasoned with your choice of the ingredients listed for the vegetable filling. Or, simply try chopped meat with tamari or oyster sauce. For a cheese filling see the cheese stuffing on the opposite page.

Punch down the twice-risen dough and knead it for a moment. Break off a small piece the size of a walnut, roll it into a ball and press it down on a floured board. Roll out the dough into a circle. Fill the baos as for moh-moh (see page 183) and set them on their twisted end.

Let the bao rise until doubled and steam as for moh-moh, 20 minutes. *Serves* 2 to 4

Filled Balep

These are cheese or meat and vegetable-filled pastries that are pan fried until golden and puffed. Delicious for breakfast, tea, or a late supper.

Dough
2 *cups flour*
½ *cup butter or shortening*
pinch of salt
1 *Tbsp. milk or more*

Cheese filling
2⅓ *cups or more grated cheese*
    (*part may be cream cheese*)
3 *cloves garlic, minced*
¼ *tsp. grated ginger*
⅛ *tsp. cayenne or* ½ *tsp. Tabasco*
1 *Tbsp. minced cilantro*

Meat filling
see filling for moh-moh
    (*page 182*)

Cut the butter into the combined flour and salt and add enough milk to make a dough similar to one for pie crust. Roll the dough out on a floured board to less than ⅛ inch thick and cut into circles 3 to 4 inches in diameter. Place a little stuffing in the center, fold the dough over, and pinch the edges together. Or, cover one piece of filled dough with a second piece and pinch the edges. Carefully roll the stuffed pastry out until it is very thin and you can barely see the filling under the top layer of dough.

Place the pastries in an ungreased heavy skillet or on a griddle over low heat and cook slowly until golden and puffed on each side. Serve hot as they are or with a spicy sauce. *Yields* 12 small cakes

Tukpa

There are as many variations of Tukpa as there are valleys in Tibet. It is a rich meat-based soup made with noodles and has a marvelous seasoning.

12 *cups water*
1 *frying chicken or more, or*
    about 3 lb. leg of lamb, or
    about 3 lb. of beef, or
    vegetable stock
3 *bay leaves*
½ *onion, chopped*
salt and/or tamari to taste
2 *tsp. minced ginger*
1 *recipe noodles (see page 108)*
1 *cup sliced celery*
2½ *cups shredded Chinese*
    cabbage or bok choy
2½ *cups shredded spinach*
½ *cup water*
4 *Tbsp. cornstarch*
1 *Tbsp. oil—aromatic sesame*
    oil is best
4 *or* 5 *cloves minced garlic*
½ *tsp. turmeric*

*You may wish to cut the meat, dust it with flour, and fry it in oil until brown—as in making a stew.

Bring the water and meat, bay leaves, onion, salt and ginger to a boil and simmer slowly for 1½ hours or until the meat is tender.* If you are using chicken, at this time you can bone it. Chop the skin into fine pieces and reserve. If there is a large lamb or beef bone, crush it and return it to the broth. Let the broth simmer with the bones until you are ready to add the noodles.

Prepare the noodle dough and cut the noodles into any particular shape that suits you. In Lhasa the noodles might be small, uniform, and thin. We enjoy a farmer's version where the noodles are made about ⅛ of an inch wide, and 1½ inches long. They cook up a bit larger and are pleasantly chewy.

Chop the vegetables. Have the water and cornstarch ready. Mix the oil, garlic, turmeric, and crushed peppers in a small pan, but don't heat it yet. Mince the cilantro.

Check the stock to see if you still have about 12 cups. If not, add a little more water and bring it to a simmer. Remove the bay leaves and the bones.

Now you are ready to assemble the Tukpa. Add the meat to the broth and return it to a simmer. Add the noodles, and when they are

1 *tsp. crushed red chiles, or more to taste*

2 *to 4 Tbsp. minced fresh cilantro (Chinese parsley) for garnishing*

about half done, add the cabbage and celery. When the cabbage is about half done and the noodles are almost tender, add the cornstarch and water. Stir. When the soup is thick add the spinach. Heat the spices in the oil for one minute and add them to the soup. If you have reserved chicken skin, chop it very finely and add it now. Let it simmer for one minute and correct the seasoning. The soup should be a bit hot from the chiles and strong in the fresh garlic flavor. Add the minced cilantro and serve it at once. This is a one dish meal.

If you are making the vegetarian version, chop hard cheese into small pieces and sprinkle it into the soup just before serving. *Serves* 6 to 8

Tibetan Saffron Rice

A delicious rice served at festivities and offered to honored guests.

1⅔ *cups water*
pinch of saffron
pinch of salt
1 *cup rice*
¼ *cup dark raisins or chopped dates*
¼ *cup golden raisins*
¼ *tsp. cardamon (optional)*
¼ *cup honey*
¼ *cup butter*

Heat the water and add the saffron and salt. Let the saffron soak for ten to fifteen minutes until the water is golden yellow. Bring the saffron water to a boil and add the rice. Stir. Let the water boil until you can see the grains of rice at the surface, then add the dried fruit. Cover and let the rice and fruit steam over very low heat until done. Toss the hot rice with the spice, butter, and honey, and serve hot or cold. *Serves* 2 to 4

Green Beans West Szechuanese

2 cups green beans, cut French
    style thinly on the diagonal
4 cups boiling water
2 Tbsp. oil
½ tsp. Szechuan pepper or black
    pepper
½ tsp. five spice powder or
    ground anise or fennel
½ cup sliced mushrooms
¼ cup sliced green onions
½ cup black bean sauce (page
    125) or canned Chinese bean
    sauce (from soybeans)
cayenne and salt to taste

Wash, trim, and slice the beans French style. Blanch them in the boiling water for 5 minutes and drain. Heat the oil in the skillet and add the pepper. Sauté the green beans in the oil with the mushrooms until tender but still crisp. Add the green onions and the Szechuanese black bean sauce. Combine the ingredients and add the salt and cayenne to taste. Serve hot. *Serves 4*

Suchi

This is a very rich and sustaining cereal with an unusual texture. Although it is traditionally served before short fasts, it is also a delicious snack. A good food to take along on a hike or camping trip. Try it for breakfast.

5 Tbsp. butter
1 cup farina or cream of wheat
1 to 1¼ cups milk
2 or more Tbsp. honey
⅛ tsp. salt or to taste
½ cup nuts
½ cup dried fruit: raisins,
    chopped dates or apricots.

Melt the butter in a small skillet or wok and add the farina. Stir the farina constantly over medium heat with a spatula. The grains will turn white and then a light gold. When the farina is golden, add the milk and continue to stir until it has been absorbed. Taste the cereal, and if it seems too dry, add up to ¼ cup more milk. Stir the cereal over low heat until it is almost dry. Add the salt, honey, nuts and dried fruit. Serve hot or cold. *Serves 2 to 3*

Mongolian Cabbage

4 *cups head cabbage or Chinese*
    cabbage diced in 1″ × 2″
    rectangles
1½ *tsp. salt*
⅔ *cup onion, diced*
3 *Tbsp. oil*
1 *cup mushrooms, sliced*
½ *cup green pepper, in strips*
½ *tsp. anise seed, or Chinese five*
    spices, or ground star anise
⅔ *cup water*
1 *Tbsp. cornstarch*
1 *Tbsp. tamari*
salt and crushed red chiles
    to taste

Dice the cabbage and spread it on a tray. Sprinkle the salt over it and roll it with a rolling pin or pound it with your fist until the salt is absorbed by the cabbage. Let it stand for 30 minutes or longer, stirring occasionally. Taste the cabbage and if too salty, pour ½ cup of water over it, drain well, pat it dry.

Sauté the mushrooms in the oil for a few minutes and add the cabbage and green pepper strips. Add the anise seed and stir. When the cabbage is tender but still a little firm, combine the water, cornstarch, and tamari and pour it into the vegetables. Stir constantly until the sauce thickens and season with the crushed chiles and salt to taste. Serve steaming hot. *Serves* 4 to 6

Khaptse

In Tibet these appear in baskets covered with red silk whenever there is a celebration, but especially during the New Year. They are a delightful doughnut-like cookie with many variations in shape and composition. The recipe that follows is for a very traditional sweet Khaptse.

4 *cups unbleached flour*
1¼ *cups sugar—for a medium*
     sweet cookie
½ *tsp. salt*
⅔ *cup melted butter*
4 *eggs*
1 *Tbsp. water*
solid shortening for frying

Mix the dry ingredients in a large bowl. Melt the butter, cool, and beat in the eggs and water quite thoroughly. Make a well in the center of the dry ingredients and stir in the eggs and butter. Knead the mixture in the bowl until all the flour has been combined and the dough is smooth.

Roll the dough out on a floured surface into a square approximately a foot on a side and ⅛ inch thick. Remove the uneven edges from the dough with a sharp knife.

First cut the square into strips that are an inch wide. Then cut the square into thirds at right angles to the strips. This cuts the strips into thirds. You should end up with pieces of dough one inch wide and about 4 inches long. Cut a slit in the center of each piece of dough. Carefully lift the piece from the board and curl one end of the dough through the slit and pull it through. Straighten the khaptse flat on the table.

A container such as a wok works best to deep-fry these because it offers more surface area and requires less shortening. Heat the fat until a small piece of dough turns golden at a

count of 30 seconds. Drop the khaptse into the fat. They will sink to the bottom and then rise. When they are golden, turn them over, fry, and drain on absorbent paper. These may be rolled in crystallized sugar, or lightly dusted with powdered sugar. We enjoy khaptse just plain, and lots of them, please.

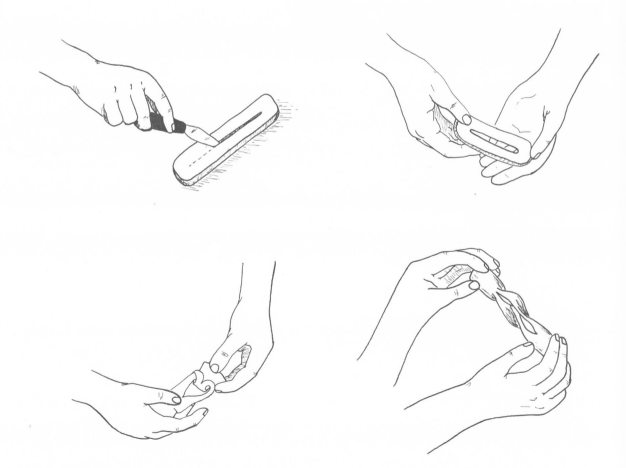

Yeasted Rice-Honey Khaptse

This recipe, believe it or not, has been inspired by a similar Italian cookie called Sfingie! These are a wonderful holiday treat.

Dough
4 *cups milk*
½ *cup rice*
1 *Tbsp. yeast*
2 *eggs*
¼ *cup water*
⅓ *cup honey or more to taste*
1 *tsp. nutmeg or cardamon*
      (*optional*)
⅛ *tsp. salt*
4 *to 6 cups flour*
oil for frying

Sauce
½ *cup honey*
3 *Tbsp. water*
¼ *tsp. cardamon, nutmeg, or*
      cinnamon and 1 tsp. almond
      and/or lemon extract

The night before you intend to serve these khaptse, bring the milk to a boil in a heavy pan over a low flame and add the rice. Simmer the rice very slowly, stirring a few times to loosen it from the bottom, for about 25 minutes or until very tender. Remove the rice from the flame, cover, and let it stand in a cool place until the following day.

Dissolve the yeast in the water for about 10 minutes. Stir the beaten eggs, honey, spice, and salt into the rice and add the flour until you have a medium stiff workable dough. Knead the dough until smooth. Pat the dough into a greased bowl, cover, and let it rise in a warm place until doubled, for one to one and a half hours. Punch the dough down, knead it for a minute and form it into a ball. Roll the dough out into a rectangle ¼ inch thick. Cut the khaptse as in the preceding recipe and fold. Let them rise about thirty minutes and deep fry until golden.

If you would like to make these cookies still sweeter, heat the honey, water, and spice to boiling and brush it on the warm khaptse. They will be a little sticky, but quite good. These cookies are also nice with the addition of sesame seeds to the dough.

Yeasted khaptse may also be baked instead of fried. Place them on a buttered cookie sheet and brush them with additional melted butter. Bake at 350° for about 15 minutes or until golden brown. *Yields* about 70

Tibetan Tea

This is a stimulating, warming, and hearty beverage. It is not our usual idea of "tea", nor is it a "soup". It is unlike any other beverage in the world. Tibetans prepare tea that is fermented and pressed into bricks. It is wonderfully aromatic and has the unique quality of becoming stronger the more it is boiled. Soda is added to this broth to sweeten it, neutralize some of the acid and to provide minerals in the diet. A little salt, milk, and fermented yak butter complete the traditional brew. The version that we offer appeals to both Tibetan and Western palates.

A salty tea may taste strange to us until we lay aside our preconceptions. This extraordinary tea is delicious any time of day and especially good when the weather is chilly.

2 cups water
1 to 1½ Tbsp. Darjeeling or other
    black tea
½ cup milk or half and half
¼ tsp. salt
½ pinch soda
1 Tbsp. butter

Boil the water and pour it over the black tea. Steep the tea about 10 minutes. Strain the tea into a blender or small saucepan and add the other ingredients. Purée the broth in the blender for a few seconds or beat it with a wire whisk. Heat the broth in a saucepan until it is quite hot, but do not let it boil. Serve immediately—and drink it slowly. Some people enjoy this tea with a little grated nutmeg sprinkled on top. *Serves* 2

Beverages and Teas

Most people prefer just one beverage with their meal, and at that a very familiar and simple one. Yet the right tea can make the difference between a table where people sit in private worlds of steaming food, and a table where people take pause to look up and savor everyone and everything with clarity and freshness. There are so many prepared herbal teas and beverages available now that it is easy to experiment; perhaps at a special tea time set aside just for that purpose. When you are familiar with the beverages which follow, it becomes possible to choose a selection for a meal and to serve them in succession to complement each course. Selecting a special beverage to serve with dessert is a simple way to transform an ordinary meal into an occasion for people to express their pleasure at dining together. Very small additions of citrus peel or spices to black tea or coffee are a subtle way to alert your friends that something special is in the air that evening, as well as in the heart of the cook.

Pure Teas

You might enjoy preparing herbal teas carefully so that their flavor is delicate, clear, and "no stronger than the water is hot." Teas are water and the flavor of the tea should be as secondary to the water as its temperature. Teas may be sipped, considered, appreciated: they are the essence of the ordinary. Unfortunately, most of us have been raised on thick coffee, oversteeped pekoe, and strong chamomile and peppermint teas that almost taste like soap. Maybe we are accustomed to too much craving. A well-prepared tea can teach us the secret of "just enough."

A tea can be made from any heab on your spice shelf. A few leaves of eucalyptus, juniper, or other wild herbs collected on a camping trip can make a souvenir tea. However, try this only if you are confident of your botany. Teas can also be made from dried fruit and berries, or fruit skins, or sprouts. Nasturtium flowers, honeysuckle, jasmine and roses can make good teas, too.

One of our favorite teas is made from dried Hibiscus flowers. In Mexico it is called *Jamaica*. The petals are soaked for a few hours in cold water and the red tea has a delightfully tart flavor. It is a good source of vitamin C.

Soy-Carob Milk

2 *cups soymilk*
2 *tsp. or less carob powder*
1 *tsp. honey, or to taste*
¼ *tsp. vanilla*
¼ *tsp. cinnamon*
a few grains of salt

Purée the ingredients in a blender. We find we like this drink with very little carob. Carob is subtle and its delicacy is lost when it is overused. Carob, contrary to popular opinion, is not a replacement for cocoa—it is a whole and distinctly flavored food in itself. This drink is good hot, but best when served quite cold. *Serves* 2

Lassi

2 *cups yogurt*
1 *cup sliced fresh fruit (mango,*
    banana, strawberries, etc.)
1 *tsp. honey—more or less*
2 *or 3 crushed ice cubes*
dash of nutmeg or cardamon

Purée all these ingredients in a blender. Garnish with a little more spice or a piece of fresh fruit. A wonderful East-Indian drink. If it is a little thick for you, add more ice cubes or milk. *Serves* 2 or 3

Indian Tea

Rich, stimulating, and heart-warming. For many of us it is the only real answer to freshly brewed coffee, particularly when we are working late into the night.

1 *cup water*
2 *Tbsp. fresh ginger, grated, or*
1 *tsp. ground ginger*
8 *whole cloves, or*
¼ *tsp. ground cloves*
3 *black teabags, or*
3 *Tbsp. black tea*
3 *cups milk*
honey to taste

Heat the water to boiling; add the ginger and cloves and simmer for 5 minutes. Add the black tea and steep for 5 minutes longer. In a separate pan, heat the milk without boiling and sweeten with honey. Strain the tea and spices into the hot milk and correct the seasonings. *Serves* 2

Nutmilk

½ *cup almonds, walnuts, or*
    cashews
2 *cups soymilk, water, or milk*
½ *cup powdered milk*
1½ *cups water or juice*
honey to taste
a few grains salt

Purée the ingredients in a blender. Serve cold or steaming hot. *Serves* 4

Hints and Secrets

Cooking in Quantity

Here are a few hints on cooking for large groups of people from a small kitchen.

Organization. By all means allow yourself plenty of time to prepare the meal. Let the excitement of the occasion increase your perception of tastes, colors, and timing. Cooking is great fun when three or more people work together. You might ask people to take responsibility for specific dishes and then make yourself available to help them out and learn from what they are doing.

Menu. Pick foods that you particularly enjoy eating *and* preparing. Select some dishes that can be made ahead of time and served cold or at room temperature, such as salads, dressings, breads, and desserts. You might choose one dish that is a little fancy and challenging, just to impress yourself. However, plan a main dish that will tax neither your time nor your stove. If it needs last minute preparation, make sure you can allow yourself time to attend to it. When your entrée can be cooked an hour before dinner and kept warm in the oven, you will have both the time and the space to prepare last minute sauces and vegetable dishes.

Recipes. Most recipes can be doubled or multiplied even ten times without requiring significant changes, except, perhaps, in spicing. However, this need not trouble you, for the rule in spicing, anyway, is to taste as you go. Rice takes less water to cook: if you are preparing over ten cups of raw rice, it is usually best to divide it into smaller pots. Otherwise, the bottom may be mushy, the middle perfect, and the top too dry. Bread will require less yeast and salt in larger batches. You may wish to undercook the vegetables slightly if they are to be held at a warm temperature before they are served.

Baking. If you crowd the oven with loaves of bread, potatoes, or casseroles, the temperature will drop considerably and the oven will take additional time reheating. Plan to schedule longer cooking time—up to fifteen to twenty minutes more for these dishes. Scorched and burned edges of food can be prevented if you can shift the food around in the oven when it is halfway through baking.

Don't get so caught up with the details of one dish that you forget to tune in to how the whole meal is progressing. Be sure to allow yourself time to appreciate all the energy that is gathering; in the kitchen, in your helpers, and in the food you are preparing.

Serving. Cooking for large groups of people usually means a celebration. Big heaping platters (and small ones, too) invite creative assembly and garnishing. When the ingredients for the garnishes have been prepared ahead of time, then you can relax and enjoy presenting the food to please the eyes, spirits, and the health of your guests.

Garnishing

The way food is served makes a big difference in how it is eaten. Garnishing is probably not an adequate word to describe the process of *presenting* a dish. More impor-tant than any last-minute touches to a platter of food is the way it is cut before it is cooked. When vegetables are prepared with the intention of revealing the beauty of their structure, it is easier to taste their distinctive flavors. The physical unique-ness of each food is appreciated with the eye; the size and structure influences its texture when it is cooked; and the degree it is cooked is often a key to its taste. When we cook with an awareness of the individ-uality of each ingredient, there is often no need to decorate the finished dish because every part of it is in artful relationship.

One way to look at garnishing is to see it as stripping away the carelessness and chaos that can attend cooking. The Jap-anese have made an art of arranging food in clear patterns just before it is served that makes the simplest foods special and delicious. When we do make final additions to a platter, they should balance the color and texture of the food. A few washed leaves or flowers placed around a dish can be a way of showing our respect for the food and for the people who are to eat it. These details can transform the food we have prepared into a gift.

Notes on Spices, Seasonings, and Ingredients

Spices add more than flavor. Many of them stimulate digestion, awaken the senses, and, like herbs in general, have a beneficial influence on the nervous system. The quality and strength of a spice varies enormously, so please season to taste! We will not attempt to list all the seasonings that we use, but rather offer notes about some of the seasonings mentioned in these recipes. If you can not grow your own spices, you may still be able to grind herb seeds as you need them. A small molineaux mill is a pleasure to use and freshly ground spices are more likely to contain all their essential aromatic oils.

Allspice: This is not an assortment of other spices but a richly evocative spice with a flavor that is distinctly its own. Allspice has a natural affinity for whole wheat. Try just a pinch in your next loaf for a richer wheat taste.

Aromatic sesame oil: This is an essence carefully extracted from roasted sesame seeds and should not be confused with regular sesame cooking oil. Aromatic sesame oil is much darker, expensive, and of course, deliciously fragrant. The brands available from Japan are more concentrated than the Chinese varieties we have tried.

Basil: (For us, the summer means peaches, tomatoes, corn—and basil). Fresh leaves of home-grown basil are a supreme treat in just about any vegetable dish and salad. Basil is easily grown in warm weather with plenty of sun and moderate water. The plant has oval shiny deep green leaves and is beautiful and also quite fragrant in a pot on a sunny windowsill.

Black pepper: Here is another important spice that is often so stale or of such inferior quality that many people think it simply hot and without a real flavor of its own. It is worthwhile to find the best peppercorns available and to grind them in a small hand mill over your food right at the table.

Caraway: While whole caraway seed is often used in breads, ground caraway is also very useful. It provides a rich and subtle 'grounding' flavor when combined with other spices in sauces, soups, breads, and dressings.

Cardamon: Like all spices, cardamon varies considerably in the quality and strength of its flavor. A good cardamon may be a little more expensive, but it is a wonderful seasoning. Try ground cardamon in fine egg breads and coffee cakes. This rich and faintly resinous fragrance is so beloved in Sweden that practically all pastries labeled "Swedish" are flavored with cardamon. This spice is also good in curry powders, and you may find a minute amount refreshing in a cream sauce over cauliflower or eggs. Cardamon also compliments peaches, apricots, and mangoes.

Celery seed: These add a sharp, slightly sweet "green" flavor to dressings, sauces, and pickles. These seeds are very potent, so use with foresight.

Cilantro: We use the Spanish word to refer to the distinctively aromatic green leaves of the coriander plant. To call it "Chinese parsley" seems to miss the boat. Cilantro is easily grown in a sunny garden from available coriander seeds.

Cloves: This spice stimulates the senses and is a good toner for the nerves. Try it in tomato sauces and in teas.

Coriander: The ground seed is also very nice in a "sweet" curry mixture. Try it in recipes with baked apples or other cooked fruits.

Cumin: Ground cumin seed provides much of the rich fragrance in a good chili powder. It is also a central ingredient in a curry mixture. When cumin is teamed with thyme it is a good addition to grain dishes.

Fennel and anise seed: These taste a little like licorice, but each have their own distinctiveness and are milder. They are often included in the Swedish rye breads and also can be used to flavor cookies. These seeds can be ground and added in very small quantities to Chinese sauces. Also try Chinese "five spices" which is a mixture of these two ingredients and other spices in the licorice family of flavors.

Foenugreek: Foenugreek seeds make an interesting tea. Ground foenugreek is an excellent addition to light curry sauces for vegetables or rice. It is especially good combined with other "curry" spices in nut-based dressings and sauces.

Ginger: Grated or minced fresh ginger root is a pleasure and can be substituted for dried ginger in most recipes. Lightly sauté it in oil for a few seconds before adding it to batters or sauces. Fresh ginger can be kept for months in damp sand.

Honey: A good natural food store will often have many varieties of honey in bulk that can be tasted for the asking. This can be an informative and pleasant experience. Our choice runs to buckwheat honey and honey produced from wild flowers of the desert areas. This latter honey can be exceptionally healthful.

Lavender: A pinch of finely minced and dried lavender adds a very nice fragrance to salad dressings, light cream sauces (with nutmeg), an occasional fruit salad (with sherry) and tea.

Miso: This is a paste of fermented beans and grains. It is a healthful addition to soups and sauces as well as a fine soup in its own right. There are many varieties available in most health food stores and oriental markets. We recommend the *Book of Miso* by Shurtleff and Aoyagi for more information and recipes.

Nutmeg: If you have a can of stale ground nutmeg—please throw it out! Whole nutmegs are available at the supermarket and can be grated quickly and easily. They are not only pleasant—they really sing. Use fresh nutmeg in breads and with fruits, but especially in cream sauces and soups.

Oyster sauce: Good quality oyster sauce can be obtained in Chinese specialty shops and some supermarkets. Use it as you would Worcestershire sauce in soups and sauces, especially in oriental dishes. This condiment has a very deep and rich flavor with a slight oyster accent. Lee Kum Kee is a good brand.

Rosewater: Rosewater can be obtained in some markets or can be made at home by bruising and soaking unsprayed rose petals in water. This is a delightful addition to custards and light fruit salads. Honeysuckle and jasmine also make delightful flower waters for teas or seasoning. Try sprinkling flower water over fine breads and cakes.

Salt: We recommend the use of sea salt because it contains many trace minerals and iodine beneficially balanced for our bodies.

Star anise: A star-shaped seed pod, star anise is ground and used in Chinese cooking. An especially pleasant and distinctly different member of the large family of the licorice flavors.

Szechuan pepper: This is not a true pepper, or even a chile. It is the dried fruit of a tree related to the "California" pepper tree, whose fruit you can also use if you are unable to obtain Szechuan pepper from a Chinese grocery. It is uniquely fragrant with a slight peppery taste. The Tibetans are quite fond of it and call it "yerma". This spice is good as a garnish on vegetable dishes.

Tamari: Although Japanese tamari is unavailable in most of this country, the term is commonly used to mean soy sauce or "shoyu", and we keep to this usage in this book. We generally select a light Japanese soy sauce in our cooking.

Thyme: Possibly the most complimentary of all spices. It is the generous spirit of white sauces and the companion of fresh vegetables.

Curry: This is a mixture of many spices. Here are four different curry powders that can be mixed in advance and added to sauces or vegetables at your convenience: *Ginger curry:* 2 parts ginger, 1 part cumin, ½ part allspice, ½ part foenugreek, ¼ part cayenne, ¼ part minced ginger; *Mustard curry:* 4 parts ground mustard, 2½ parts cumin, 1 part nutmeg, ½ part cayenne, ½ part turmeric, ½ part cardamon; *Rich curry:* 2 parts cumin, 1 part caraway, 1 part foenugreek, 1 part allspice, 1 part mustard, ½ part turmeric, ½ part cayenne; *Sweet curry:* 1 part cinnamon, 1 part nutmeg, 1 part cumin, 1 part cardamon, 1 part ginger, 1 part turmeric, 1 part cayenne, 1 part cloves, ½ part fennel or anise.

Kitchen Knives

We have found that it only takes three different knives to do all the cutting and chopping in a vegetarian kitchen. These are: a paring knife with a blade about three inches long, a bread knife with a serrated blade, and a French knife with a blade from eight to ten inches long. The French knife is a particularly unique and valuable instrument. It is a Chinese cleaver that has been modified with a slightly curved blade and a tapered, pointed end. The curved tip is an advantage because when it is pressed against the board it becomes a pivot that enables the center and base of the cutting edge to be brought down on the vegetable sharply and firmly. The whole knife becomes a lever with a fulcrum that moves up and down the blade with each cutting stroke. Because one part of the blade is always resting on the board, chopping can be quiet, rhythmical, and very precise. If you will try to use the French knife in this way, vegetable chopping can also be very fast.

A sharp knife is an extension of the cook's mind. When the body, blade, and senses are coordinated one can actually "feel" the texture of anything that is sliced. As the edge of the blade moves through fruits and vegetables, revealing the small miracles of internal structure, the mind and sense are also sharpened and balanced. Many people find when their attention is focused in this way that vegetable chopping becomes an invigorating and relaxing experience.

Knife Sharpening

A dull knife hacks, mashes, and fights. A sharp knife can be a delicate extension of sight and touch.

When sharpening a knife, always hold the blade at a 15° angle to the stone. Move the knife along the stone so that the blunt side (top of the knife) precedes the cutting edge (bottom of the knife). Place the cutting edge nearest the handle on the stone and guide it across the surface to sharpen the blade from the handle to the tip. Turn the knife over and repeat this process in the opposite direction, again with the back of the blade leading the cutting edge.

We use three different stones to bring very dull blades to adequate sharpness. First sharpen the dullest knives on a coarse man-made stone to bring the cutting edge to a proper bevel. The second step is to further refine the cutting edge on a natural Washita stone. The final honing is done on a natural Arkansas stone. Most people will find that a single Washita stone can sharpen their knives adequately. We have found that although carbon steel knives need more sharpening than stainless steel knives, they require less time and effort to sharpen. Very light machine oil should be used on most stones as you sharpen the knife, although the manufacturers of some man-made stones will recommend that you use water.

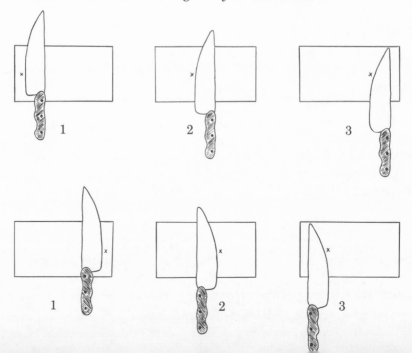

Index